CERVANTES

CERVANTES

BY

WILLIAM J. ENTWISTLE

OXFORD
AT THE CLARENDON PRESS
1940

OXFORD UNIVERSITY PRESS
AMEN HOUSE, E.C. 4
London Edinburgh Glasgow New York
Toronto Melbourne Capetown Bombay
Calcutta Madras
HUMPHREY MILFORD
PUBLISHER TO THE UNIVERSITY

PRINTED IN GREAT BRITAIN AT THE UNIVERSITY PRESS, OXFORD
BY JOHN JOHNSON, PRINTER TO THE UNIVERSITY

CONTENTS

THE THEME

CERVANTES is Everyman's private discovery. Every healthy boy delights in the adventures of *Don Quixote* with the frank hilarity of youth, but this is not to discover Cervantes. That comes later. To enter into the fullness of the first and best of novels requires experience in the reader to match that of the writer. An art of dialogue is necessary, an exchange of impressions of life; the reader must bring his own enthusiasms and his own disappointments under the tolerant half-smile of the battered veteran of Lepanto, the ex-slave and organizer of escapes, the entangled civil servant, the prisoner, the writer of genius who had no reputation until grey hairs were on his head, and who remained for the rest of his life 'old, a soldier, a gentleman, and poor'. And when the discovery is made there is so often a sense of astonishment in the discoverer. How is it, one exclaims, that he should pass for an untutored genius who gathered doctrine from all sources and formed so notable a philosophy of life? How is it, says another, that those who are puzzled by the strength and weakness of Spain fail to find the food of social meditation in the revelation given by the book? How surprising that the world does not recognize in the Manchegan the embodiment of strict justice? or, it may be, the *reductio ad absurdum* of chivalry? As each new discoverer has his own quota to add there can be no end of books about Cervantes, nor of surprise at what has been so strangely overlooked. It is in keeping, therefore, that this essay also should express surprise: surprise that, in all the mass of Cervantine publications, so little interest has been shown in the man at his job, his job of book-maker.

For whatever Cervantes may have had to say about justice, chivalry, reality, or frustration, he was first and always a maker of books. Fate and inclination drove him to it; fate stopped all other outlets for his genius, and inclination made him stoop to recover even the torn papers in the streets. The first we hear of him is as an earnest student of rhetoric. Though he deserted Apollo for Mars, honourable wounds drove him back to the more peaceable wielding of a pen. The torments of the bagnio and the fierce struggle to be free did not silence a tongue ever ready to indite a sonnet for a friend or find relief in appeals to Our Lady. Several kinds of public service he attempted as an alleviation of the intolerable poverty of the literary life, and indeed he seems to have gained his living mostly by the performance of fortuitous commissions. These chances, and some quality of his own mind, made his output irregular and his methods of composition spasmodic and repetitive; but the tale of his works steadily grew. The indifference of publishers and actor managers, no matter how brilliantly alluring the promises he made them, blocked his way to meet the great public, which was quite unaware of his supreme genius for close on sixty years; when it could no longer be doubted, the reward remained meagre. Only an overmastering creative passion could have held Cervantes to his desk in the face of such disappointments, but in obscurity and poverty he elaborated his thought and his style into something unique in world literature.

This long history of patient craftsmanship has been overlooked in the light of one blinding paradox. Despite his assiduity, his care, and even his genius, there is an immense amount of Cervantine writing which no one willingly reads. How is it that the author of *Don Quixote* is also the author of the *Galatea* and so many mediocre copies of verse? Is his genius an accident? Is he a hollow thing through which a great inspiration has passed?

'Let us not hesitate to say it: without the *Don Quixote* and some *Novels*, all Cervantes' other works would not probably be known to-day save by mere erudites and specialists; none of them was such as to compel the attention of posterity. *Don Quixote* is an accident, a lucky stroke, a flash of genius, a miracle in the literary life of Cervantes. Before that date he had attempted almost all the genres; in several he had failed and in others had scored a mediocre success. He failed to understand himself, for it seemed he had never clearly realized the immense superiority of his masterpiece.'[1]

It is not a complete answer to retort that the same mind is expressed in the famous and in the obscure works, since that leaves the paradox still standing. Dr. Castro's book on Cervantes' thought[2] is the most significant and suggestive in recent years, and it would be almost conclusive were we dealing with a moralist or a pedagogue. He has shown that Cervantine texts may be pinned against

[1] E. Mérimée, *Précis d'histoire de la littérature espagnole*, Paris, 2nd ed., p. 277.

[2] A. Castro, *El pensamiento de Cervantes*, Madrid, 1925.

an Erasmian pattern, with no more than the incon-
sistencies inevitable to one who had no occasion to
unify his doctrine into a system. In Cervantine
thought there is no difference between greater and
lesser works, but the same optimistic doctrine of
Nature's workings faced by the same disenchant-
ments in actual experience. There is no greater
pedagogue than Cervantes, who has a recipe even
for falling in love. But unified as his thought may
be, it was his main endeavour to amuse and entertain; and on so many occasions we are not amused.

Dr. Castro's work, however, points towards the
right conclusion. If Cervantes took such care to
gather and propagate sound doctrine concerning
society and character, he took equally great pains
with his art. His style was deliberately formed for
his purpose of honest entertainment, and it has the
same ingredients when it succeeds as when it fails.
There is overwhelming evidence of care and plan-
ning, despite the ebb and flow to be noted in his
output. Few writers can have worked harder than
Cervantes did in his fashion, and we may decidedly
reject the notion of accident or wayward inspiration
in his moment of triumph. There is consistency
and purpose in his art as in his thought.

We enter the right path when we notice that the
terms of the paradox have been too sharply put.
Whatever grounds we have for including some
Exemplary Novels in our count of the best works
and excluding others are valid also for and against
different sections of *Don Quixote* itself. Taken as a
whole that work is a masterpiece comparable only
to itself; but it is a mosaic of parts of unequal

interest. The affairs of conventional shepherds are not more welcome in it than in the pastoral *Galatea*, and the history of Cardenio and Dorotea abounds in improbabilities. On the other hand, as good a naval battle can be encountered in the *Galatea* as anywhere in Cervantes; the first act of *The happy Ruffian* and a handful of scenes from *The Traffic of Algiers* are among the truest things he wrote. His genius is unequal in all his writings, and what detracts from the appeal of his first book diminishes also the interest of his last. Yet last and first, if we read with patience, there are moments or periods of the authentic inspiration.

Two things which hampered Cervantes were his lack of certain endowments and the false suggestions of contemporary aesthetics. He lacked the lyrical gift, yet he prized poetry above all the other arts. To the drama he brought the talents of a novelist, and there was none to set him right. The aesthetic principles admitted in that age were a confused mumble from Horace and Aristotle, not to mention the fag-ends of medieval rhetoric; in so far as any accent rose above the rest it was that of 'imitation', and Cervantes strove to earn merit by 'imitation', though his genius impelled him to an entirely new creation. It was only when success came that he could take the measure of his individual achievement; and even then his work was misconstrued. *Don Quixote* was received with hilarity, but not with the respect due to an artist, and after this immortal work was done Cervantes sat down to achieve a good repute from the learned by imitating the manner of Heliodorus! The thrust of his genius was, indeed, irresistible, but it was made against clogging inertia without and within.

This genius was the genius of an exemplary novelist. What the term means will have to be defined in a later chapter; the unit of construction is the short story or novelette, and the moral intention requires contact, variously maintained, with observed conditions of life. His plays have dimensions and plots like those of the exemplary novels, cover the same years of creative activity, and may be reckoned to be warped expressions of the same genius. All his longer novels are resolved into episodes which are exemplary novels. These latter were not written in the year of their publication (1613), nor were they all collected in the book entitled *Exemplary Novels;* their number is more than doubled by additions from *Persiles* and *Don Quixote*, and their composition covered thirty years of intermittent effort. They represent the chief effort of Cervantes' life, and it was as one of them that the great novel began. *Don Quixote* opened a richer vein than Cervantes had ever before explored and infinitely transcended its origins, but it differed less in kind than in amplitude. It was a flash of genius, no doubt, or rather a glow deepening into a steady light, but it was not an accident in the literary life of its author. He required, like all others, the felicity of a rich idea; but when it came, long years of training had given him style, method, and experience capable of exploiting it to the full.

EXPERIENCE

Puras verdades já por mim passadas.

IN several of Velázquez' pictures in the Prado Museum the original lines are beginning to show through the paint. They bear witness to change of design in one or two cases, but never to faults of drawing. Whatever could be observed and placed on canvas was faultlessly rendered by Velázquez, though he lacks the same sureness of touch when he is forced to rely on imagination (as in the movements of horses), and his groups often fail to cohere. A similar sureness of observation is found in Zurbarán, and Murillo at his best, as well as in a great part of Spanish literature. There is no lack of conventional or idealistic effects in either Spanish painting or literature; but it is the realism which stands out. It is not merely that characters and incidents are like life, but they seem to be actually parts of life. The author, we are convinced, must have known an individual Celestina or Lazarillo. It is the same with Cervantes. His habits of thought and methods of construction are often conventional, and he is liable to cut personages out of pasteboard to fit prearranged situations; he is not at home with the gentry, and uncertain when treating of good women; but he floods his pages with incidents which, we feel, must have been true, and entrusts his plots to a swarm of picaros, peasants, minor gentry, scullery-maids, and sinners who could have been identified in the flesh by those who knew him.

Such realism puts a premium on the biography

of the author. The best, perhaps the only illuminating commentary on his work must have been the record of his own experiences; and it happens that these can be known with some fullness, thanks to his troubles and the legal papers which they engendered. There is nothing substantial to be added to the fully documented biography by the late James Fitzmaurice-Kelly;[1] but the comparison of this study and the data of the works offers some surprises. Many of Cervantes' experiences are not reflected, or only dimly, in his writings. There is nothing to correspond to the long series of documents affecting his squalid daughter's affairs, and indeed nothing that happened to him after 1600 had a formative influence on his genius. On the other hand, the events of his youth and early manhood are disproportionately influential. He must have read most of the books that inspired *Don Quixote* more than ten years before he put pen to paper. There are also experiences which, almost certainly, did not happen to him, and yet bulk largely in their literary effects. We know little of his schooling, but there is a clear impression of life at Salamanca University in half a dozen of his stories. Flanders, visited by his elder brother but not by himself, forms part of his scheme for a young man's career.

In short, it is plain that the experience of life

[1] J. Fitzmaurice-Kelly, *Miguel de Cervantes Saavedra: a memoir*, Oxford, Clarendon Press, 1913. R. Schevill, *Cervantes* (Master Spirits of Literature), London, Murray, 1919, is of equal authority and wider scope. Professor Schevill discusses the works as well as the life.

which is revealed by Cervantes in his writings is on the one side more narrow, on the other wider, than the events of his own career. In bygone days this circumstance led to many false conjectures from those who sought to infer his biography from his novels. Even where the basic experience is one and the same, as in the case of the sea battle which preceded his captivity, its artistic presentation may be multiple, and thus unreliable as to detail. To clear away these encumbrances from the story of his life has been the task of the documentary biographers ; but having ascertained the facts as accurately as possible, it is necessary to return to the fictions in order to accomplish that object for which the biographies were undertaken, viz. to show the effect of experience upon creation. The lives of poets and men of letters are significant for their effect on their works, just as political biographies gather importance from political events. Apart from his creative genius a poet or novelist is as other men are, or perchance a little less. Measured by such consequences, second-hand and even bookish experience may prove more relevant than portions of the authorized biography.

Our first glimpse of Cervantes is as an excited spectator of Lope de Rueda's farces. Lope de Rueda, the founder of professional acting in Spain, died in 1565, when Cervantes was eighteen years old, and the novelist records that he was buried between the two choirs of Córdoba Cathedral, near to the famous madman Luis López. Where the encounter took place is not known, but the most plausible date is 1561, when Cervantes was

fourteen and Rueda was offering a series of entertain-
ments in Madrid. The effect was indelible. The
boy was filled with a love of stage-plays and players
which did not leave him for the rest of his life;
his mind was formed to simple contrivances and
entertainment based on single scenes, without a
closely knit plot; and in particular he grasped the
technique of the curtain-raiser, as we might call it,
used as an interlude (*entremés*) between acts. As a
master of the interlude Cervantes is the successor
and perfecter of Lope de Rueda. He felt the
enchantment, however, not merely in that part of
stage-craft which he was qualified to master, but
also in a passion for the drama which ran contrary
to his gifts. For a quarter of a century Cervantes
struggled to achieve success on the stage, without
fully understanding the improvements due to later
writers. He continued to apply, partially or wholly,
an art of composition not far removed from that of
Lope de Rueda, despite the disappointment that
came from an increasing measure of unsuccess.

'A few days ago I found myself in a group of friends
talking of Comedies (this was in 1615), and things concerning them. They made such subtle distinctions and
refinements, that methought they reached utter perfection.
The question was also raised as to who first in Spain took
them out of swaddling-clothes, exposing them under an
awning bedecked with gala attire. I, as the oldest there,
said I remembered performances by the great Lope de
Rueda, a brilliant actor and a man of sound sense. He was
a native of Sevilla, a gold-beater by trade, that is, a maker
of gold leaf. In pastoral poetry he was wonderful, and
unequalled then or since in this style. And though I was
then a boy and could not rightly judge the excellence of

his verses, I find what I have said to be correct with respect to some lines that stick to my memory (re-examined at my present mature age). Were it not to exceed the limits of this prologue, I would reproduce some to prove the truth of the judgement.

'In this famous Spaniard's time the whole baggage of a comedian actor-manager went into a single sack, being four white sheepskins ornamented with gilt leather, four beards and wigs, and four crooks more or less. The Comedies were conversations in the bucolic style between two or three shepherds and a shepherdess. They were improved and expanded by two or three interludes—farces of the negress, the ruffian, the clown, or the Biscayan, all four and many other parts being played by the said Lope with all the skill and propriety imaginable. At that time there were no stage effects or challenges between Moors and Christians on foot or on horse. No figure emerged or seemed to emerge from the centre of the earth through the understage. The stage was formed of four benches set square and four or six planks on them, rising four palms above the ground. Nor did clouds descend from heaven with angels or souls. An old blanket moved two ways on cords was the adornment of the theatre, corresponding to the present vestuary. Behind the blanket musicians sang some old ballad without guitar accompaniment. Lope de Rueda died, and, being an outstanding and well-known person, was buried in the cathedral of Córdoba (where he died) between the two choirs. The famous madman Luis López is also buried there.

'Lope de Rueda was followed by Navarro, born at Toledo. He was famous in the part of the cowardly ruffian. He somewhat advanced the adornment of the Comedies, altering the sack of clothing to boxes and trunks. He brought the singers from behind the blanket into the public theatre, and removed the beards from the comedians (because up to that time no one had played a part without a false beard), and made all play bare-faced apart from the roles of old men and such as required disguise. He invented effects, clouds, thunder and lightning, challenges and battles; but in this respect he did not reach the present sublime height.'[1]

How soon Cervantes may have begun to tread in Lope de Rueda's steps is not known. In *The Bagnios of Algiers*, which may have been composed about 1592–6, he opens his third act with a performance of one of the master's farces, probably the lost *La Gila*. He states that Spanish slaves obtained a few days of grace in the Christmas season, and after the performance of mass would fall to improvising some such performance. If there were a demand, might there not be a supply? Cervantes would not have been slow to take the opportunity. However, we have no record of such an activity, since only a few personal and complimentary verses survive from the years 1575–80, and our witness only says that Cervantes penned odes to the Virgin. The interludes which Cervantes sent to the press in 1615 are mostly of seventeenth-century date, though some bear the marks of his acquaintance with Sevillan roguery in the last decade of the sixteenth.

In his three- and four-act plays Cervantes employs a technique beyond that of Lope de Rueda. Rueda's longer performances consisted of strings of scenes only loosely gathered into a plot, and interrupted by farcical sketches. Cervantes uses a formula held in common with the Sevillan Juan de la Cueva, whom he is careful not to mention, as Cueva did not mention him. It included the improvements attributed above to the Toledan Navarro, together with a regu-

[1] Prologue to *Eight Plays and Eight Interludes*.

lar division into acts, and the principle of polymetry.[1]
In his more ambitious plays Cervantes is not an
imitator of Rueda.

We may, however, associate with this encounter
his unflinching fondness for stage-folk, and his
repeated assurances that they are necessary to the
public weal. In *Licentiate Glass* his commendation
is, perhaps, a trifle stilted, but in *Pedro de Urdemalas*
(of about the same date) not only does he make his
hero an actor, but he pronounces a discourse on
the art which is worthy to be set beside that of
Hamlet. The happiest of these theatrical sketches
is that of the unnamed stage-poet of *Persiles*, iii. 2.
He was busy patching a play on Cephalus and Procris,
having 'been forced by necessity to exchange Parnassus for inns, and Castalia and Aganippe for the
ponds and rivulets of the highways and hotels'. No
sooner had he set eyes on the pretty heroine than
he saw her as a handsome page, a nymph, a queen.
Hearing something of her story, he at once began to
weave it into a plot, and was puzzled as to how
to supply the necessary buffoonery. He urged her
to join the company, and wear gaudy clothes and
receive the attentions of the young bloods. Only

[1] *Polimetria* is a term used in Spanish criticism to describe the
use of different types of verse in a single composition. Under
the hand of Lope de Vega polymetry was the means of adapting the
metre to the rise and fall of dramatic emotion, but in the epoch
of Cervantes it had no such propriety. The principle of uniformity
on the French classical stage requires of a single metre totally different emotional effects, and not always successfully. In Shakespeare
and Ben Jonson variety is gained by mingling prose and verse. The
Greeks and the Spaniards have obtained the necessary variety by
varying their verses.

marionette shows displeased Cervantes; he held that puppet-players were rogues, and such indeed was the one whose entertainment Don Quixote so decisively ruined.

The education of a young man of spirit is a recurrent theme in Cervantine prose. After several years spent at the University of Salamanca, either in the brilliant manner of the aristocracy or with the diligence of the poor, the young man would pass to Italy and Flanders, to complete his knowledge of life and art. This curriculum is supposed, not merely for characters expressly so described, but incidentally for many others also; and Cervantes goes so far as to share the Salamancan misprision of 'provincial' universities, such as Osuna and Sigüenza. His motives were deeper than those of the Cockneys who, on one day of the year, are divided into Light and Dark Blues; for student life at the University of Salamanca was indubitably an experience, though vicarious, of our author. He had studied the undergraduate, with his practical jokes and his logic-chopping. The disputatious habit is exemplified by the 'nego-probo' of the students in *Love's Labyrinth*, and in *The Cave of Salamanca* one of the fraternity repays lodging in a straw heap by affecting to conjure up a supper and two devils to serve it, thus helping on a love intrigue. Two undergraduates, wishing to see Italy and the wars, but too poor to travel at their own expense, buy a picture of Algiers and go begging alms as if they were returned captives. In the *Persiles* (iii. 10) Cervantes shows that there were country provosts too alert to be deceived by this naïve roguery, but too indulgent not to help forward the youths' laudable ambition.

The protagonists of *Lady Cornelia* are Salamancan students who have gone to finish their studies at the Spanish College of Bologna; but these are aristocrats, and they are treated conventionally. It has always seemed different with *Licentiate Glass*. Tomás Rodaja, a poor Andalusian boy, was determined to educate himself at Salamanca. Two young gentlemen took him there as a sizar, and he acquitted himself with high distinction. Making a favourable impression on Captain Diego de Urbina, he accompanied a Spanish detachment to Italy, which he traversed from north to south. He also saw something of Flanders, before returning to complete his professional education in Spain. Stricken mad by a love-philtre, he was followed by the boys in crowds as dense (according to our author) as those which accompanied a popular professor. He criticized all classes of society, using the stock reproaches against doctors, lawyers, courtesans, and the like; but his attitude was, none the less, the one normally adopted by his creator. His enthusiasm for the legitimate stage, his praise of good poets, his dislike of puppet-shows, his suspension of judgement as to divination and medicine, and his doubts concerning married honour, identify him with his author. What, then, of his university career?

There are many gaps in the early portion of Cervantes' biography, so that we cannot wholly exclude the notion of some residence at Salamanca. As an experience it counts for as much in his writings as the years of imprisonment at Algiers; and yet it was most probably experience at second-hand. Cervantes was indebted for an education to the Studium of Madrid and its high-master, López de Hoyos. He appears as a ' dear pupil ' of that master in 1569, and is authorized to speak on behalf of the school. As he would then be twenty-one years of age, the term ' dear pupil ' is open to various conjectural interpretations. Was he a former pupil or still *in statu pupillari* ? Did he begin late ? Was he a pupil-teacher or junior master ? There is nothing to show which of these interpretations is correct, but the context shows at least that his studies were of rhetoric, both in his native language and in Latin, and that they extended as far as the original composition of verses on set themes. Dr. López de Hoyos was himself addicted to these exercises in academic elegance, and he was by profession a Latinist. His studium would rank to-day as either a grammar school or a university Arts Faculty. One entered the University of Salamanca at the age of eleven (Tomás Rodaja) or fourteen (Fray Luis de León), and the first stages included the rudiments of rhetoric and Latinity. But the later developments of the Salamancan curriculum are not to be seen in Cervantes. The logic of Calderón, the theses defended and controverted, the apparatus of authority, and the predominant interest in theology, are wholly alien to Cervantes; and very few books issued from Salamanca would fail to come beneath the lash of the first prologue to *Don Quixote*. Quite unlike the Salamancan scholastics, Cervantes was also subtly different from the humanists, such as Fray Luis de León or Sánchez de las Brozas. He knew something of their attitude to life, and he reproached them for concealing their poetical talents.[1] But his own outlook was more generously human, and of an older growth than theirs.[2]

Cervantes' teacher, Dr. López de Hoyos, was a cautious admirer of Erasmus.[3] He was acquainted with the *Antibarbarorum liber*, the *Exomologesis*, and the *Apophthegmata*, on his own admission, ten years after the Holy Office had begun to condemn the writings of Erasmus in Spain. Such condemnations did not imply the disappearance of the books or authors involved, nor was Erasmus systematically banned until the *Index* of 1612. When completing the second part of *Don Quixote* in 1614, Cervantes

---

[1] *Parnassus*, iv. 325–45. Naturally the reference might be to others, but the cap fits. The Salamancan poets concealed their work as poets, because they occupied responsible positions in the Church. The tenth of Apollo's ordinances is ' no poet must despise admitting the fact '.

[2] Or the same. Dr. Castro writes, in the article next cited, 'Cervantes, in his special domain, has the qualities of a contemporary of Montano, Luis de León, el Brocense, Sigüenza and Mariana, and many others little known to us. They all form the marvellous and heroic group which is illuminated by the dubious reflections of a melancholy autumn light. If we are to understand them, we must not make use of an ingenuous clarity and simplicity. Times were difficult, especially for those who, by travel and contact with more refined people in Italy and Flanders, were drawn by their education, genius or impulses towards freedom of thought, a thing felt the more necessary at a time when the commonweal was beginning to go downhill.' The special domain of Cervantes was not theology and philosophy, and his free use of supposedly first principles, without reference to authority, sometimes makes his reasoning more akin to that of the brothers Valdés.

[3] A. Castro, ' Erasmo en tiempo de Cervantes ', *Revista de Filología Española*, xviii, 1931, pp. 329–90.

suddenly bethought him of Fr. Felipe de Meneses' *Light of the Soul* (*Luz del alma*), a work which had not enjoyed much circulation for several years. Meneses intended to correct the ignorance of the Spanish monks and friars, and he drew heavily on Erasmus' *Encheiridion*. Erasmianism is the backbone of Cervantes' education. To it he owes his dogmas about Nature, conduct, and art; but still more is he indebted for the freedom to make up his own mind by reference to principles which seem axioms of common sense. It is an important part of his endowment. Erasmus belongs to all the world; Cervantes shares his universality.

From Dr. López de Hoyos we may suppose Cervantes learned the rudiments of rhetoric and of Latin. He shows later a layman's knowledge of the Roman poets, whose commonplaces he quotes, though not always with exactitude. His familiarity with the Italian language and literature presumably came later, during the years of his soldiering in Italy and Sicily (1569–75). He learned the common tags used by soldiers in the mixed Spanish-Italian jargon of the hostelries, splashing them, for instance, on the early pages of *Licentiate Glass*. More than that, he acquired a bias towards Italian such that he is seldom reluctant to adopt neologisms from that language. He could read with fluency enough to prefer originals to Spanish translations, and to become a passionate admirer of Ariosto, Boiardo, Pulci, Guarini, Giraldi Cinzio, Bandello, Tasso. Tasso's *Gerusalemme* seems to have been the last great Italian work to attract his admiration, and it came too late to influence *Don Quixote*. *Don Quixote* is, however,

a remodelled *Orlando Furioso*, quite as much as a revised *Amadís*. From Leone Ebreo's *Dialoghi di Amore*
Cervantes conveyed the doctrine of love largely
expounded in his *Galatea*, and there he mentions
' an aged shepherd whom they at once recognized
as old Thelesio ', and who may have been the Nea-
politan humanist Bernardio Telesio, Campanella's
master, or Antonio Telesio, recipient of a Latin ode
from Garcilaso.[1]

Acquaintance with Italy is revealed in *Love's
Labyrinth*, *Lady Cornelia*, *Licentiate Glass*, and *Per-
siles*, iv. In *The liberal Lover* Cervantes displays
his knowledge of the Sicilian waters, with their
perpetual risk of piracy. What he has to say of
Bologna and Padua in the first two works cited does
not necessarily reveal first-hand knowledge, but in
Licentiate Glass and *Persiles* the author follows a well-
marked road to Rome. In the former the stages are :
Genoa, Lucca, Florence, Rome, Palermo, Messina,
Naples, and Rome again, Loretto, Ancona, Venice,
Ferrara, Parma, Piacenza, Milan, Asti. Complaint
has been made against the traveller that he should
have shown so unintelligent an appreciation of
Renaissance Italy. In Genoa he saw the harbour
and sampled Italian wines, and noted that the girls
had fair hair ; at Lucca he was aware of hospitable
treatment in the inn ; he cast no more than a glance
at Florence, ignoring the art collections ; the description of Rome might have come from a guide-
book, and that of Venice is a dull commonplace.
In *Persiles* the travellers follow a similar route :
Milan, Lucca, Acquapendente, Rome. In the one

[1] A. Castro, *El Pensamiento de Cervantes*, Madrid, 1925, p. 163.

case it is a poor scholar who travels, in the other a prince ; but the intellectual interest is no greater in the second journey. It is adorned with a mention of the Accademia degli Intronati, but at a distance ; an incident involves painting ; and there is a lush adventure with Hipólita, a Roman courtesan. But that is all. What Cervantes' characters get from their travels is doubtless what he himself obtained, travelling without favour or introductions : the sight of men and cities, but, apart from later reading, no knowledge of their minds. Of the educative value of even so limited an experience he had no doubt. His own travels did not extend to Flanders, with its vast mercantile wealth and endemic war, but he might have learned something of that country from his elder brother Rodrigo.

His military service lasted for five years. His share in the battle of Lepanto was a source of legitimate pride, since he received 'a wound which, though it looks ugly, seems to him beautiful, as having been obtained on the most memorable and lofty occasion known to the past or likely to be seen by the future, while he was fighting under the victorious banners of that thunderbolt of war, Charles V, of happy memory'. His left arm became unserviceable, and he also suffered wounds in the chest. Companionship in this battle and in letters linked him affectionately to Andrés Rey de Artieda and Cristóbal de Virués. Concerning the battle itself Cervantes has recorded no clear recollections, though he may have developed the theme in his lost play *The naval Battle*. He gives details about the affair of Navarino in 1572, when the Spanish com-

mander failed to trap the whole Turkish fleet at
anchor, and he was especially impressed by a fine
feat of arms by Don Álvaro de Bazán, the Spanish
Nelson. Memories of this engagement are preserved
in his semi-autobiographical *History of the Captive
Captain*, inserted in *Don Quixote* i (39–40). The
same passage describes the loss of La Goleta and El
Fuerte in the year 1574, and *The liberal Lover* implies knowledge, though not necessarily intimate, of
the expedition against Cyprus. Of the great battle,
however, there is no clear impression, though its
incidents are doubtless recapitulated in his ode on
the Invincible Armada. Anxiously expecting news
of the fleet he had helped to provision, Cervantes
imagined the excitement and disasters of a sea-fight
in the fullest vividness of detail, harking back no
doubt to his last experience of decisive war. The ode
forms a curious contrast to Fernando de Herrera's
Ode to Lepanto, perhaps the greatest political poem
in the Spanish tongue. As an account of the action
that ode is worthless, and it does not even correspond to the conditions of any modern action. The
Song of Moses over the drowned Egyptian Chariots,
the Lament for Tyre, and a couple of Psalms were
gathered by Herrera to make a statement of Spanish
theocratic nationhood, with all the sombre mag-
nificence of Vulgate latinity transposed into the
weightiest of the vernaculars. The event is trans-
fused by the heat of language and imagination; but
Cervantes, with better knowledge and a more gallant
patriotism, lacked the finer lyrical gift.

A great series of sea battles runs through Cervantes' works; it is the engagement of Les Trois

Maries, in which he was enslaved in 1575. The bare fact is made verse in the *Epistle to Mateo Vázquez* in 1577:

> 'Twas in the galley *Sun* that there went down
> my fortune's radiance, in my despite
> involving others' ruin with mine own.
> Valour and dash at first we showed in fight,
> but later grim experience convinced
> us of futility and lack of might.

The passage is repeated as the personal history of the soldier Saavedra in *The Traffic of Algiers*, and Ricaredo, of *The Spanish Englishwoman*, was also taken at Les Trois Maries, his vessel being hemmed between two Turkish corsairs, though the action of that novelette begins in 1596 and extends over a decade. In *The liberal Lover* there are abundant memories of the same action. The hero is captured off the coast of Sicily and held for a while on the island of Pantellaria, and he engages in another sea-fight in the Aegean before the plot can be concluded. The affair was being developed and varied to suit Cervantes' creative convenience. It attains its fullest development in the fifth book of *La Galatea*, in the narrative of Timbrio's homecoming from Italy. The passage is too long to cite in full; but it would serve to convince any reader that Cervantes had even in 1585 attained maturity as a master of prose narrative. Fifteen enemy vessels made the assault; there was a furious rush, a desperate defence of the cabin where two ladies were voyaging, and the bitterness of capture. A violent storm the next day, of a kind Cervantes must have experienced not infrequently, wrecked their captors on a Christian shore and gave liberty to the prisoners.

In the beginning of *The Bagnios of Algiers* another history of enslavement is related. The opening scenes show a Barbary raid on the Valencian coast with telling effect. A similar raid gives matter for *Persiles*, iii. 11. These are doubtless the experiences of others, though Cervantes, out of his own memories, was qualified to add accessory details.

His captivity extended over five and a half years. We know that he bore it with a dauntless courage that wrung admiration from his captors. He organized escapes tirelessly, and on one occasion concealed, fed, and at last protected with his own life a large number of slaves in a garden. When disaster had reduced all to one level of misery, Cervantes stood out by his daring, courage, and genius. He played the role of counsellor assigned to the soldier Saavedra in *The Traffic of Algiers*. In that play and the identical lines sent to Mateo Vázquez he urged Philip II to use the unmeasured might of Spain to destroy this nest of pirates and release 15,000 or 20,000 captives; and it would have been well for Spain had Philip listened to the ablest of her sons. *The Traffic of Algiers* is full of attempted escapes, and the Spaniards in it keep up a farouche standard of daring. A desperate attempt to reach Oran is probably a transposition of one of Cervantes' own experiences, and the escape through Hassan's garden in *The Bagnios* is another of his projects, successfully accomplished. These plays have plots which fail to cohere, but in isolated scenes are of the greatest vividness. The scene of the slave-market in *The*

Traffic is poignant in its contrast between childish prattle and the stoical despair of their parents. Equally convincing is the insolence of the little renegade. Perhaps the scene rang too true to be bearable, for in *The Bagnios* it was replaced by a conventional scene of child-martyrdom.

In 1581 Cervantes was dispatched on a short mission to Oran. It was there, doubtless, that he gathered material for his vivid representation of an attack on the Oran forts in *The gallant Spaniard*, together with the outlines of his hero's career. The rubrics of the play assert that the hungry Buitrago, who had a pious device for augmenting his rations, was taken from life.

A number of figures came to Cervantes as parts of his experience in captivity. There was the gallant renegade from Spain, Morate, and the cruel Greek Yzuf. Arnaut Mami and Dali Mami the sea-rovers, and the more famous Barbarossa, are also persons he delights to reproduce. The imagination of a novelist, working on the data of life, provided Cervantes with plots more or less true to Algerine life. One that pleased him greatly was the plot of the 'crossed lovers'. A betrothed pair are taken prisoner and become slaves in the same house. The master of the house falls in love with the maiden and seeks the mediation of the youth; the mistress loves the youth and seeks the intervention of the maiden. Thus the lovers can plead their own cause in the name of their master and mistress. Discovered embracing, they still contrive to cover their love until, at last, a chance comes for escape. A second plot is that of the 'captive captain'. A Spanish captain's noble bearing in the bagnio wins the heart of a Moorish girl, who communicates secretly through her window. They contrive to escape, and she turns Christian. Then there is 'the boy in the harem' and several situations to display the valour of uncompromising Christianity. The plot of 'the crossed lovers' was used to bind together *The Traffic of Algiers* about 1585, and also the novelette *The liberal Lover*. It appeared again in *The Bagnios of Algiers*, in combination with that of 'the captive captain'; and the second plot functioned alone in *The History of the captive Captain*, inserted in *Don Quixote*. 'The boy in the harem' is used in *The Grand Sultana* as a sub-plot, and again, somewhat vaguely, in *The History of the Moor Ricote* in the Second Part of *Don Quixote*. Catalina de Oviedo in *The Grand Sultana* and Saavedra in *The Traffic of Algiers* are examples of stubborn Christianity on a heroic scale; Madrigal, in the former play, displays the same quality on the level of buffoonery.

The knowledge of Moslem life which he acquired at first hand in Algiers he applied at second hand to Oran in *The gallant Spaniard*, to Cyprus in *The liberal Lover*, and to Constantinople in *The Grand Sultana* and the lost *Traffic of Constantinople and death of Selim*. In these pieces his hand is less sure, and the conventional portrayal ascends to farce at some moments. The inverisimilitude of *The Grand Sultana* ruins what might have been a powerful play on the conflict of two wills. Cervantes' romanticism was always prone to run away with him, and yet it is true that for the early years of his literary life this Algerine experience was his surest guarantee of truth. It served to give substance and life to his work until his studies in the picaresque brought his realism to its zenith.

Having returned to Spain in 1580, Cervantes knew many changes of domicile. His brother accompanied the Spanish troops into Portugal that year, and he also followed. Between 1580 and 1587 he was normally stationed in Madrid, but in the latter part of 1587 he was commissioned to collect wheat for the Armada under the orders of Diego de Valdivia in Sevilla. Sevilla became his centre for about fifteen years. The failure of the Armada left him unemployed, and he vainly solicited an appointment in Bolivia. He continued to collect public moneys under conditions of increasing difficulty. In 1588 he had suffered excommunication for one unlucky attempt to collect wheat; in 1591 and 1592 he was heavily in arrears of pay, and at the same time his own books were falling into disorder. We hear of him at Teba, Écija, and Granada, and he suffered imprisonments in 1592, 1597, and almost certainly in 1602. Removing to Valladolid when that city became the capital of Spain in 1602–8, and accompanying the Court to Madrid in or about the latter year, Cervantes had unusual opportunities to know the roads and cities of Spain, and especially the great metropolis of Sevilla; the more so since his travels as a man probably duplicated other wanderings as a child in the company of his father, an errant surgeon.

It is this vagabond existence on the Spanish roads—'those roads of Spain that one sees everywhere and are nowhere described', as Flaubert said

—that gave Cervantes his formula for the novel. The late Sr. Unamuno declared that for a novel it sufficed to take two characters and set them talking. For Cervantes it sufficed to take two persons and put them on a road. On a road any adventure was possible. 'Long journeys [he wrote] always bring with them a diversity of events.' Novels of chivalry, it is true, were fought out on the highways and byways, and the Greek novel on which *Persiles* was modelled was a romance of travel; but in adopting the same procedure for the *Exemplary Novels* Cervantes was revealing his own hand.

Two main roads are involved. The last of his novels, *Persiles*, takes a west–east route across central Spain. Travelling slowly from Lisbon, at the rate of two or three leagues a day, the travellers entered Spain at Badajoz. Passing near Trujillo they reached Guadalupe, where ended the episode of Feliciana de la Voz. Thence they went to Trujillo, and so on to Talavera at the time of the festival of La Monda. They proceeded to La Sagra, north-north-east of Toledo, characteristically avoiding the city. Turning south-east they crossed the Tagus near its junction with the Jarama, and passing through Ocaña they came to Quintanar de la Orden. This is the point of intersection of the two routes used by Cervantes. Juan Haldudo the rich was a native of Quintanar de la Orden : Don Quixote and Sansón Carrasco must have been his neighbours, since it was from a herdsman of Quintanar that the bachelor had bought the dogs Barcino and Butrón to serve for the pastoral eclogue planned beside Don Quixote's last couch. It was in Quintanar that there ended the episode of Antonio the barbarian, one of the main strands of *Persiles*, with its curious likeness to Cervantes' own circumstances. Antonio was a poor gentleman and a soldier. He had served in the German wars, but was treated with disrespect on his return to his native village by a young aristocrat. He had been addressed as *vos* and not as *vuestra merced*, the normal usage among gentlemen. The result had been a quarrel and long years of exile. A similar story is told of Don Fernando de Saavedra, hero of the play *The gallant Spaniard*. A document, dated 15 September 1569,[1] orders the arrest of one Myguel de Zerbantes for having wounded at Madrid a certain Antonio de Sigura; this Zerbantes had been sentenced to the loss of his right hand and ten years of exile. Nothing forbids identifying him with our author.

From Quintanar the travellers proceeded to 'a township, neither very small nor very big, the name of which I do not recall'. The phrase resembles that which opens *Don Quixote* : 'in a township of La Mancha, the name of which I do not care to recall'. Whether they are the same, of course, is one of the undiscovered secrets. Don Quixote's native place must have been near El Toboso, the home of Dulcinea. Azorín estimates that 'near' in La Mancha implies a distance of two kilometres ;[2] but there is no village satisfying that requirement. It must have been within a day's ride of Puerto Lápiche, and within easy distance of Campo de

[1] J. Fitzmaurice-Kelly, *Miguel de Cervantes*, Oxford, 1913, p. 16.
[2] Azorín, *La Ruta de Don Quijote*, Buenos Aires, Losada, 1938, p. 104.

Criptana, where the windmills are, and Quintanar. These are conditions very imperfectly satisfied by Argamasilla de Alba, the favourite of tradition.[1] From Argamasilla to Puerto Lápiche involves ten hours of travel. Azorín reached Criptana by train. El Toboso is three hours distant from Criptana. Argamasilla de Alba would have been a convenient starting-point for the third sally, since it is only eight hours' ride from Ruidera, and two more ('two leagues' according to Cervantes) from the famous caves of the Guadiana. The Campo de Montiel lies still farther to the south, and certainly the hero, sallying forth southwards into the Campo de Montiel, would not have reached Puerto Lápiche in the north-west; nor having reached Puerto Lápiche in the north-west, would he have returned home via Quintanar in the north-east, without some other night spent on the road. The fact is that if Cervantes does not recall the name of Don Quixote's home town, it is because no town corresponds to his entire convenience, and he had no particular site in mind. As for the township indicated in the *Persiles*, it must have been situated on the road from Quintanar to

[1] Rodríguez Marín further argues that Argamasilla de Alba did not then lie on the north-south road used by Cervantes, and that Argamasilla de Calatrava, to the south of Ciudad Real, must have been intended. Don Quixote must have passed through it on his return from the Sierra Morena, and may have lodged there. But the site adds at least forty miles to distances which are already too big. See the argument in the edition of *Don Quixote*, Madrid, Tip. de la Revista de Archivos, 1927–8, vii, appendix vi. Cervantes himself contributes the name Argamasilla only as the site of the Academy whose members wrote the verses at the close of the First Part.

Valencia. The next place marked is a fork, leading
to Cartagena on the right and Valencia on the left.
Presumably this is the fork just south of Albacete.
Valencia was the eastern terminus of this journey.

The road from north to south was of greater importance in Cervantes' novels. He knew Valladolid
intimately, and also Madrid. The road descended
to Toledo through Illescas and La Sagra, or followed
a more direct line through his wife's property at
Esquivias to Ciudad Real. A third route crosses the
Tagus at its confluence with the Jarama, at Aranjuez,
and forks left at Ocaña for Quintanar, and right for
Puerto Lápiche. A left fork at Quintanar through
Alcázar de San Juan enables travellers to avoid the
defile of Puerto Lápiche by joining the Córdoba
road at Villarta. Knowledge of Valladolid is shown
in *The illustrious Kitchen-wench* and *Tricked into Marriage*, of Toledo in the former, and of Madrid in
The little Gypsy and *The Voyage to Parnassus*. South
of the Tagus lies the territory of Don Quixote, so
admirably described by Azorín in *La Ruta de Don
Quijote*.

The roads form the sides of an 'A', on the bar of
which Don Quixote's home must have lain, together
with El Toboso and La Criptana. His point of
departure has been fixed by tradition at Argamasilla
de Alba, but the indication is doubtful. During
the first sally Don Quixote rode into the Campo
de Montiel, lying many leagues to the south of his
home, and then surprisingly reached the inn of
Puerto Lápiche in the north-west. It forms part
of a village that straggles down a broad pass in the
olive-clad Sierra de Villarubia. When next we hear

of the knight he is in the act of returning home by the eastern leg of the 'A', near Quintanar. The site is fixed, not only by his meeting with Haldudo of Quintanar, but by the fact that the merchants who discomfited him were on their way to Murcia. We must connect with this fact the circumstance that, though the author gives details only of the night at the inn, the housekeeper and niece speak of an absence of three days.

The second sally began in a westerly or north-westerly direction, towards La Criptana. It is (says Azorín) 'a white city, lying hugely on a slope and illuminated by the blood-red rays of the evening. On the top of the hill the windmills slowly turn their wings; the plain extends beneath, ruddy, monoto-nous, blank.' From this point the hero reached the western leg of the 'A' at a point not specified, and the greater part of his adventures occurred at the unknown inn adorned by Maritornes. He turned southward, and must have passed through Ciudad Real without incident. Argamasilla de Calatrava must also have lain on his route, and may have afforded one of the inns for his adventures. Cer-vantes is careful not to mention the place where Don Quixote entered the Sierra Morena, but Sancho thought of evading the Holy Brotherhood 'by traversing the whole of it and emerging at Viso or Almodóvar del Campo' (*Don Quixote*, i, chapter 23). The main road entered the Sierra after leaving Almodóvar del Campo, and then traversed the Valle de la Alcudia. Here stood an inn, El Molinillo, where Rinconete and Cortadillo first met, and four leagues away there was the inn of La Tejada or

Tajada, celebrated for the beauty of the wench Marinilla (the model of *The illustrious Kitchen-wench*). Farther to the south the road excites no remark as it passes through the Guadalquivir valley to Sevilla. Five leagues to the north of that city and off the main highway lay Castilblanco, the scene of part of *The two Damsels*.

Don Quixote's third sally was across country. He proceeded first to El Toboso, and then south-eastward along the Guadiana to Ruidera and the Caves. Then he struck north-eastward towards Zaragoza, over hilly ground. The stages go unnoticed, though they probably included Cuenca and Calatayud. The ducal residence, the scene of so many chapters of the Second Part, was presumably the seat of the Villahermoso family at Pedrola, near the Ebro. From Pedrola Don Quixote descended the Ebro, avoiding Zaragoza, and took the main road to Barcelona.

Not only do these roads play their part in his novels, but the barren and desolate monotony of La Mancha was (according to Azorín)[1] a necessary condition of the great novel. The inhabitants of Argamasilla were first settled at Moraleja. A pestilence drove them to Boñigal and another brought them to Argamasilla.

'Do you see how the mind of a new generation, among whom was Alonso Quijano, was created in a few years between 1555 and 1575? Do you see how the panic, the nervous anxiety, the exasperation and anguish of the mothers of these new men was communicated to them and formed in the new town an atmosphere of hyperaesthesia

[1] Azorín, *La Ruta de Don Quijote*, p. 33.

of the senses, of restlessness, of perpetual longing for the unknown and distant? Do you now realize that all Argamasilla is a town-errant, and that the greatest of knights-errant had to be born here?'

And again :

'My hack plunges on with impetuous desperation. The broad strips succeed each other with monotonous equality. The whole plain is grey and uniform, without a hillock, without the slightest undulation. In a moment the sown fields have dropped behind, with early wheat or barley touching the furrows with green, and now all the plain embraced by our sight is a grey, grubby, desolate extension.' 'Along this road, across these plains, precisely at this hour one burning July morning, passed the great Knight of the Sorrowful Countenance. It is only by crossing these plains, soaking in this silence, enjoying the austerity of this scenery, that one learns to love with complete intimacy and depth this tragic figure.'[1]

The great empty spaces were perhaps more populous with travellers than at the present day. There was no train to rush them screaming through the night from Madrid to Sevilla or Valencia. They had to proceed by easy stages and on foot. There were muleteers going to Sevilla with their lights o' love, and cloth merchants descending to Murcia. A troop of recruits would be marching to Valencia or a train of galley-slaves to the arsenal at Cartagena. There were mountebanks displaying puppets, and members of the Holy Brotherhood policing the public ways. Ladies and gentlemen would pass with their gaudy attendants, for one wore colour on the roads. Sombre cortèges moved by night

[1] Ibid., pp. 74 and 75.

with candles and litanies. Returning captives from
Algiers would tell their adventures in the inns,
and students would beg alms by pretending to be
captives. A motley company would be huddled
round the fire of the despicable hostelries, under
the presidency of a host ' more thievish than Cacus ',
together with his wife and daughter and a kitchen-
wench of surpassing ugliness or (peradventure)
beauty. Each little village had its priest and barber,
making company for the local gentry by right of
wit and learning. And there were the Dulcineas
and Sanchos and Teresa Panzas and Sanchicas. In
fact, here on the roads of La Mancha was the heart
of Spain, known only to Cervantes. He and others
with him were acquainted with the rogues of the
towns and the affected gentlemen ; but he alone
knew the common people.

His roads form, as we have seen, a huge cross on
the face of Spain. The ends of the cross were, so
to speak, blobbed ; for each had special interest for
Cervantes. The western end lay in the city of
Lisbon, which he probably did not know, for his
praise of its site is conventional. The eastern end
might be either Valencia or Barcelona. Valencia
served as the emplacement of Moorish assaults.
What impressed him most in Barcelona was the
endemic brigandage in the hills, the most curious
feature of which was its pretence to gentility. In
the second book of *La Galatea* he speaks of ' the
ancient usage of that kingdom, that when people
at feud are persons of quality, they go out to the
company of bandits and injure each other as much
as possible, both in life and property, which is

contrary to all Christian custom and worthy of censure'. On this datum he builds an exciting episode of his subplot. He is more specific in the Second Part of *Don Quixote* (Chapter 60) in speaking of the Niarros (or Nyarres) and Cadells. The famous Roque Guinart belonged to the Niarros, and there is a strange conversation between two men of their hands, Don Quixote and the bandit, in which the former advises Roque to cure the sickness of his conscience by using the same daring in the service of chivalry. They part with mutual respect, and perhaps it was not Don Quixote who was most to be pitied. Closely akin to this use of the Catalan feuds in the service of fiction is the conclusion of *The two Damsels*, where again Roque intervenes to procure a not too probable solution. He is also mentioned in *The Cave of Salamanca*. En Perot Rocaguinarda was at the height of his fame in 1610, but was subdued in the year following, and embarked with many of his followers for exile on 21 July 1611. Apart from this use of Catalan banditry Cervantes associated Barcelona with memories of the harbour and service of galleys, with the tempestuous crossing to Genoa, and with the disorders of its populace.

His knowledge of Sevilla was of supreme moment in his art. It was in Sevilla that he enriched his insight into character by wide and kindly study of metropolitan rascality. He enriched his language by copious draughts of the vernacular and even of thieves' slang. He learned how to make action proceed from character and to make truth intrinsic, not adventitious, and he laid aside for a while his

harmful romanticism. In all this he may have followed the lead of Antonio Álvarez de Soria, the
ruffian poet, who was executed in 1603. Quevedo
mentions his fame, but Cervantes does not. He
might have had reason to approach the topic with
caution, for D. Francisco Rodríguez Marín[1] believed their friendship to have been so intimate that
Cervantes left a memorial to his friend in the Loaysa
of *The jealous Extremaduran*. Dressed in coloured
silk stockings with tight shoes, white or black according to the season, in serge or mixed cloths, with
small hats and exaggerated linen, rakes met in rings
and arranged the affairs of the suburb,

'marrying virgins and unmarrying the wedded wives, making
remarks about the widows and taking note of the single,
without sparing nuns; giving credit to patents of nobility
and inventing lineages, exciting rancour and burying good
fame, frightening all and astonishing not a few, offering
much, performing little; they may be brave though they
do not look it, and for this I praise them, since valour is
not a thing of appearance but of action.'

This Antonio Álvarez de Soria was a poet, and
the inventor of the curtailed rhymes which became
a mode about the time of his demise. Cervantes
uses them in the preliminaries of *Don Quixote* for
Urganda's epistle. In thieves' jargon it is necessary
to avoid certain words, and one of the devices
employed was to pronounce only one syllable. The
device was used for poetry more jocose in intention
than in effect. Antonio Álvarez had also a genius
for vituperation, and led the attack on the Duke of
Medina Sidonia in 1596 and on Lope de Vega in

[1] F. Rodríguez Marín, *El Loaysa de El Celoso Extremeño*, Sevilla.

1603. Cervantes wrote spirited sonnets against the Duke, and was supposed to be the author of the sonnet against Lope, receiving in reply from one of Lope's champions an abusive sonnet in curtailed rhymes. In short, there is strong, though not con- clusive, reason to believe that Cervantes must have known this personage in the years of his notoriety between 1595 and the end of the century. The figure of Cristóbal de Lugo, in *The happy Ruffian*, may have resembled him even more closely. How- ever this be, the ruffians named by Cervantes in *The illustrious Kitchen-wench* are Alonso (for 'Gon- zalo ') Genís, who was executed without appeal on 11 October 1596, and Ribera.

The widowed Ruffian is a candid and not unsym- pathetic study of the type. *The happy Ruffian* repre- sents in the first act one of the young bloods who imitated the baser bullies, by attacking the police, bullying shopkeepers, and consorting with persons of ill fame. Loaysa is of the same class. In *Rinconete and Cortadillo* we have, on the one hand, a sym- pathetic study of two little pickpockets and card- sharpers and, on the other, a picture of the organized crime of the city. The latter is a state within the state, centred on a ' fence ' named Monipodio. He may not have regulated his anti-republic with the efficiency that Cervantes implies, but there seems no reason to doubt that the person and his house were authentic. He is mentioned again in *The Dog's Colloquy*, where the whole range of metropolitan roguery is revealed. Gipsies lived on the fringe of this urban vice, and Cervantes, after mentioning them in the *Colloquy*, offers completer pictures in

The little Gipsy and *Pedro de Urdemalas*. The innkeeper of Puerto Lápiche is a retired rogue from
Sevilla, and his creator takes the opportunity of
outlining the geography of rascality.[1] Don Diego
de Carriazo and Don Tomás de Avendaño, in *The
illustrious Kitchen-wench*, are amateurs of roguery,
and had Cervantes completed the *Life of Ginés de
Pasamonte* which he mentioned in *Don Quixote*, i. 22,
we should not have had to judge that unconscion-
able rogue merely by the episodes of the galley-
slaves, Sancho's ass, and the puppet play.

The northern end of the cross lay in Valladolid
and Madrid, passing through Toledo. These cities
are all scenes of his novels, and display some details
of his geographical knowledge; but they came too
late in his career to count for much in the development of his art. In the Madrid period the only new
note is a genial appreciation of his own fame. He
enjoyed the opportunities to meet his contemporaries
on the Prado and by the fountains of Cibeles and
Castellana, or in the theatres and academies and the
Paseo de San Felipe. He enjoyed both fame and
seniority; for he was the 'Adam of the poets' as
the *Parnassus* avers and could (according to the
prologue of the *Eight Comedies*) cast his mind farther
back than any. Strangers came to see him from
France and were much surprised that he should
not be maintained at the public cost in the Pry-
tanæum. The young poets, like Pancracio de Roncesvalles, solicited his opinion; and one student
(Cervantes loved the *naïveté* of the student class)

[1] See appendix viii, vol. vii, of Rodríguez Marín's edition of
Don Quixote.

greeted him after his last journey with ‘Yes, indeed, this is the sound one-hander, the famous everything, the cheery writer and, to conclude, the joy of the Muses’.

Fame was sweet, but it did not yield much daily bread. Cervantes was ‘old, a soldier and gentleman, but poor’. He lived by precarious commissions when not on his wife’s bounty, and these commissions, as the soldier in *The careful Guard* admits, were not easy to obtain. He might, no doubt, have been overbidden by any subsacrist for the favours of a kitchen-wench. A dull note of hunger runs through his work. The *Numantia* is horrible rather than tragic on that account. Buitrago in *The gallant Spaniard* is consumed by eternal famine. The greater number of Apollo’s instructions to poets deal with their hungry condition. Cervantes was glad to sell his *Eight Comedies* for anything they would get. As late as 1614 he was a person of no financial consideration, nor would Apollo offer him a seat on Parnassus; he invited him to double his cloak and sit on it, without caring to notice that Cervantes had none. Nor was this his only source of anxiety. It has always been thought that the marriage-weary soldier of *The Divorce Court Judge* represented its author.

At the age of fifty-five he described his own appearance, and published the description ten years later in the prologue to the *Exemplary Novels*.

‘Him you see here, with an aquiline countenance, chestnut hair, open and clear forehead, cheerful eyes and well-proportioned curved nose; with a silvered beard, which was golden twenty years ago, large moustaches, small mouth, and teeth neither big nor small (for he has only six, and they are in bad condition and worse placed, since they do not correspond); with a middling body, neither large nor small, a lively colour nearer to white than brown, somewhat heavy in the shoulders and not very light on the feet'

—this was Cervantes. Don Quixote resembled him in age, being about fifty, and in his high colour; not to mention a certain dryness of the wits which Cervantes had felt in himself during incarceration. Don Quixote's sane counterpart, Don Diego de Miranda, 'seemed to be about fifty years of age, with few grey hairs and an aquiline countenance, his look was a mixture of the cheerful and grave, and from his clothes and bearing he seemed to be a man of worth'.

The last experience of Cervantes' life was death. If the approach of death could not count for anything in his art, it was at least the cause of some of his most moving lines. It was with a whimsical smile that the dying man received the excited homage of the student at the Bridge of Toledo, the one all agog with hope, the other about to say good-bye to wit and jesting and all good company, 'for I am slowly dying and hoping to see you soon happy in another life'. 'Yesterday they gave me the extreme unction, and to-day [19 April 1616, N.S.] I write this dedication; the time is short, the pains increase, hopes wane, and yet I carry on my life beyond my wish to live'; but he would have liked to publish the second part of his treasured *Galatea*, together with a book of short stories and a sort of heroic epic, and other 'relics and glimpses' of his soul.

SWEET POESY

Desde mis tiernos años amé el arte dulce de la agradable Poesía.

CERVANTES made his first bow to literature in the
disconcerting attitude of a prize pupil. Dr.
López de Hoyos, Latinist of the Madrid Studium
or High School, patted the head of his 'dearly
beloved pupil' Miguel de Cervantes and congratu-
lated him on his use of the 'colours of rhetoric'
and the application of a 'quite elegant style' to
'things worthy of memory'. The sonnets, quintets,
and epistle which he contributed, on behalf of the
whole school, to the master's *True History and Rela-*
tion of the Illness, happy Passing and sumptuous funeral
Exequies of the Most Serene Queen of Spain, Isabel de
Valois, in 1569 include only one false rhyme and
two false scansions. They express the inevitable
thoughts in the most obvious terms. A song is
'sad', a soul 'blessed', a height 'lofty', the earth
is 'base', glory is 'perpetual', and one hears of
this 'earthly weight'. The commonplace thought
and the banal epithet continue to be the marks of
Cervantine verse during the next fifty years. Precept demanded them, and Cervantes complied with
precept. His rhymes are bought in the cheapest
market and abound in past participles, infinitives,
and artificially accented pronouns. Such work was
not likely to draw attention when new poets were
numbered in hundreds. Three hundred competed
for a prize in Mexico a few years later. In the
homeland it was necessary to distinguish between
good and bad poets if the number was to be kept
within reasonable bounds; but even so, Cervantes

included 97 in his *Galatea* and about 150 in his *Voyage to Parnassus*.

The verses, however, are not entirely wasted. They bear witness to their author's study of good models. In 1569 there were not many to admire. Fray Luis de León wrote what may have been his first original poem in that year, and Fernando de Herrera was working on problems of style in Sevilla; but there were only two models current in print and generally admired, namely, Garcilaso de la Vega and Diego Hurtado de Mendoza. The latter was selected for an apotheosis in the sixth book of the *Galatea* under the guise of a pastoral funeral. But the influence of the former was more potent and permanent, and in these early verses it was even followed beyond the frontiers of discretion.[1] From Garcilaso he obtained a vocabulary docile to the new Italian metres, together with a fluid and generally unembarrassed manner. To what his model provided he added the ornamental epithet, which, if it did not itself give true poetry, had a certain dignity and eloquence. In his epistle to Cardinal Espinosa he speaks of the ascent to heaven of the blessed soul, the Catholic king's sorrow and need of friendly comfort, and God's choice of hardy

---

[1] Garcilaso had written *Oh, hado esecutivo en mis dolores*, 'Oh fate that takes effect in my sorrows', referring to the death of his lady. Cervantes used the phrase as if, by itself, it could mean the death of a lady:

> *A ti, gran Cardenal, yo le presento,*
> *pues vemos te ha cabido tanta parte*
> *del hado esecutivo vïolento.*

('I present it to thee, Oh great Cardinal, since we see that you have had so great a share in the violent fate-that-takes-effect.')

souls for trial. There may be nothing new in this, but it is grave, it is courageous. Cervantes was already a man to resist and overcome misfortune.

It is this instinctive gallantry which gives worth to many of his poems. It is found in the *Epistle to Mateo Vázquez* of 1577, repeated in Saavedra's monologue in *The Traffic of Algiers*. The epistle opens with a characteristic echo of Garcilaso, and then contrasts the Secretary of State with the slave. Vázquez had been born in Algiers during his mother's captivity; in 1569 he had been in the service of Cardinal Espinosa, and since 1573 he had been in direct attendance on Philip II. Cervantes soon passes in his thoughts from the mood of prostration; he speaks of his services at Lepanto and his capture in battle, and he goes on, in respectful and manly tones, to urge the king to use the immense power of Spain to destroy the nest of pirates and set free twenty thousand Christian souls. The king is at peace, his power is unbounded, the gold of the Indies flows broadly into his coffers. His father's example is before him, all men look to see the Spanish sails; who can doubt that he will prove benignant to the captives' prayer?

Philip never came, and again Cervantes misjudged him in 1588. He was at that time collecting wheat for the Invincible Armada in Andalusia, so that the expedition was not only a national, but a personal, interest. It drew from him two odes. The one is inspired by conflicting rumours of its progress. Cervantes drew on his memory for pictures of battle: flying balls, ensanguined waters, floating corpses, shattered yard-arms, tackle, keels, planks.

In his optimism he could not picture other than a victory; but his next ode was inspired by shattering defeat. Cervantes is magnified in defeat. He claims that the English victory was a gift of the winds and waves. The wounded lion returns more violently to the attack. Philip commands the resources of all the world and will be stung to vengeance by the piracies of Drake. Medina Sidonia should remember his famous ancestor Guzmán the Good, and Parma should be a second Don John of Austria. He ends exultantly:

> Oh Spain, oh king, oh soldiers of renown!
> enlist, command, obey, for heaven (I feel)
> must aid at last and help our righteous zeal,
> though in the early days it seems to frown;
> a righteous cause and resolution—see—
> enclose for us the joy of victory.

How bitterly he may have resented the king's sloth and pusillanimity we cannot know, though we may readily imagine. Medina Sidonia's cowardice and incompetence soon became proverbial in Sevilla, and rose to fantastic heights in 1596. When Essex descended on Cádiz, the Duke took measures first to protect his own house and then to vex Sevilla with war exactions. A certain Captain Becerra ('yearling calf') raged through the streets of the metropolis with his press-gang, and then, when the English had gone quietly away, Medina Sidonia entered Cádiz in pomp and triumph.

> Another Holy Week we've had this year,
> mounted in July by sodalities
> which the rude soldiery call companies;
> which not the English, but the people fear.

Of plumes and feathers was there such a store
that in a fortnight filled with hubbub rare
both dwarfs and giants fluttered in the air
and their tall edifice crashed to the floor.

The Bullock bellowed, strung them on a chain;
earth thundered and the heaven grew dark and drear,
and universal ruin threatened us;

and prudently, at last, when it was plain
Essex had gone, in Cádiz, without fear,
entered Sidonia victorious.

There is not much of this kind of verse in Cervantes, and this sonnet (recovered only in 1778) has been questioned. But there is enough elsewhere to show that when Cervantes could forget the 'colours of rhetoric' he had, after the years spent in Sevilla, another style, vigorous, biting, picaresque. It is in the same years that a similar change comes over his prose. Whether the picaresque enrichment were due to friendship with Antonio Álvarez de Soria is not to be known, but it is probable. That poetical ruffian invented the device of tailless rhymes which Cervantes (who must have known him) and Quevedo (who did know him) adopted for a season. Its source was the thieves' slang of the Andalusian metropolis. It was from them that Cervantes drew the vigorous expressions of his poetical interludes (*The widowed Ruffian*, *The Provosts of Daganzo*) and of his best exemplary novels. It was an advance in general style rather than in poetry proper. Satire rarely rises above the prosaic level, and nothing in these poems gives the sense of sudden liberation of the whole being which we expect from true poetry. But if Cervantes had formerly been eloquent and grave, now he could be incisive and sardonic; once he had exalted the ideal, now he could pitilessly uncover the real.

He was credited with having written odes to the Virgin during his captivity, but they have been lost, except for a fragment in *The Traffic of Algiers*. Some lines to St. Theresa seem chiefly evidence of incapacity for such themes. His doctrine of Nature excluded the miracle as a normal event. He accepted it only under protest and in deference to documentary evidence. Such evidence exists (he says) and gives ground for assenting to the remaining miracles of the Spanish saint. Similarly, in his prose descriptions of Loretto and Guadalupe it is the votive offerings, tangible evidence, that he notices, and in *The happy Ruffian* he alleges texts drawn up by responsible persons to justify the absurdities of the second and third acts. Accepting the miracle with reluctance, he is still further from feeling the mystical glory behind the miracle.

During many years Cervantes' friends were unable to publish books without a prefatory song or sonnet by our author. These are completely banal, and not even proof that he had read the books. They help to fix his dates and mark his associations, especially with the Lepanto group and Juan Rufo, Don John's panegyrist. Cervantes varies the obvious plaudit with the conceit. Of the conceit a desperate example is the ode he contributed to Antonio Veneziano's *Celia* in 1579, in which everything is done to torture the approximation of Celia to 'celestial', and of Algerine slavery to love's bondage. Echoes pleased his ear, as they did Cicero's. He would have been glad to write *O fortunatam natam me consule Romam*, and his plays pullulate with similar infelicities. These echoes occur as frequently in his prose, but with a quite different effect. In prose they conduce to eloquence, and to the peculiar resonance of the Cervantine period.

The piece which, among all his verses, most pleased Cervantes was the brief ballad of *Jealousy*. It saw the light in 1593 and was three times repeated in contemporary anthologies. A long way after Ariosto, it develops a decorative allegory of the lair of jealousy. By accident posterity has paid more heed to another similar ballad, *Love's Shipman*, because it happened to be included in *Don Quixote* (i. 43). Bishop Percy translated it, and through him it came to the notice of Europe in company with more authentic ballads.

Either of these ballads might have been used for the promised second part of the *Galatea*, for the pastoral novel is simply an extension of occasional erotic verse. The verses were doubtless written first, and then a prose narrative woven round them to give a background for the hints in the lines. This must have been the case with the *Desperate Lover's Song* in *Don Quixote*, i. 14, which gave rise to the story of *Grisóstomo and Marcela* in the two chapters immediately preceding. The verses suggested a disdainful lady and despairing lover, and the story presents them in the flesh; but it fails entirely to cover the data of the canzon.

The *Galatea* is a vast compendium of verses of all sorts and shapes. There are songs, elegies, eulogies, debates, satires, in all possible combinations

of line and stanza, and the quality of the workmanship, as distinct from inspiration, is high. Nothing,
however, holds our attention. Even at its weakest
the Cervantine prose is superior to his verse, and
the reader of the *Galatea* skims rapidly over the
poems to continue with the thread of narrative. But
the latter also is poesy; it is a dream world of art
in a perfected nature.

The *Galatea* is a truly surprising phenomenon.
At the age of thirty-three it was necessary for
Cervantes to choose a new career, and as he had no
specialized ability he chose that of literature. He
brought to it a remarkable experience of life.
During his wandering childhood he must have
learned much of Spain and its inhabitants, but he
had also had some good schooling. He had had a
glimpse of ecclesiastical luxury; he had fought
honourably in the decisive battle of the age. He
knew the Mediterranean and Italy. He had suffered
the bitterness of defeat, the long martyrdom of
slavery, the thrills and disappointments of attempts
to escape, the narrow avoidance of death by torture,
the wild joy of freedom, the high hopes of the return
to friends, and the cold douche of indifference.
All these things he knew—and he set about writing
a pastoral novel, without real people or life or events!
No experience, no reality enters into a pastoral
novel; not even the simplest natural happenings
enter unchanged. The day does not dawn, but
'rosy Aurora leaves the arms of withered Tithonus';
and 'fresh collations' take the place of rustic meals.
No one notices the sheep, unless at the end of a
long ode one needs a pretext for a siesta. The

unprofessional conduct of little Bo-Peep would pass with Cervantes.[1] It is not as if the ways of real shepherds were unknown to him, for no one has better marked the abyss that separates Arcadia from the country-side.

'I say that all the thoughts I have mentioned and many more caused me to note the difference in traffic and exercise between my shepherds and the others in that district and all those I have read about as practised by shepherds in books. When my shepherds sang, the songs were not well composed and melodious, but *Cata el lobo dó va, Juanica*, and other things of the sort, and that not to the sound of flageolets, rebecs and bagpipes, but the noise of one crook beating on another, or of tiles held between the fingers. They sang not with wonderfully delicate and sonorous voices, but with hoarse accents, so that together or singly they seemed to be screaming or growling. Most of the day was spent picking fleas or mending sandals. Among them there was none named Amaryllis, Phyllis, Galatea or Diana, nor Lisardo, Lauso, Jacinto or Riselo, but all were Anton, Domingo, Pablo or Llorente. So I came to understand what I suppose all men believe, that all such books are only well imagined and well written, to amuse the idle without any semblance of truth. Had it been otherwise, there would have been some survival among my shepherds of that most happy state of life, with its pleasant meads, spacious woods, sacred hills, fair gardens, clear streams and crystalline founts, together with those honest and well-phrased proposals, with the shepherd swooning here and the shepherdess there, and here the sound of a flute and there of a flageolet' (*The Dog's Colloquy*).

Well imagined and well written. The essence of entertainment is diversion, literally being turned

---

[1] MANFREDO. Where is the flock?
PORCIA. I guess I've lost them (*Love's Labyrinth*, i).

away from our normal traffic. Garcilaso de la Vega, another soldier, was famed for three pastoral eclogues; and Sir Philip Sidney for a novel. Another *Arcadia* came from the pen of Lope de Vega, though he had taken part in the terrific experience of the Armada. The age of struggle and disaster bred a longing for ideal calm; the clang of arms was only too often heard above the babbling of the brooks. The ideal worked with peculiar mesmerism on the optimistic mind of Cervantes. In his thought it always triumphed over the real. It represented free creation in art and natural perfectibility in life. By the exercise of reason, developed by education, it was possible to live after the principles of Nature, God's Vice-Gerent. This had been the happy lot of those who lived in the Age of Gold, or of the first couple in Paradise. Let the world retrace its steps and return to blessed simplicity. Let it neglect its manifold chores and vexing activities, and rejoice in the Utopian *dolce far niente*, with cheerfulness as the reigning emotion and passion diminished to an elegant swoon. Let all that is disagreeable be eliminated from the landscape; let there be no beetling cliffs, storms, deserts, or raging torrents. Let there be only 'honest and well-phrased proposals' amid the 'pleasant meads, spacious woods, sacred hills, fair gardens, clear streams and crystalline founts'.

Novels of chivalry were another branch of this literature of escape. Love was the motive of both classes of romance, but in the pastoral it led only to discourse and song, whereas it spurred knights into action. The knight might swoon at the sight of his lady, but he rarely sang; and he usually rushed forth headlong to slay a felon or fall into a magician's snare. His motives were lofty, but they smacked of a reality which Cervantes knew to be false. The pretence that such books could be a practical guide for soldiers, still maintained in the fifteenth century, was intolerable in the late sixteenth; but they did serve to raise to the nth power the usual flirtations of the salons, feats of the lists, and triumphs of battle. In due time Cervantes came to write his novel of chivalry, and drew together the bonds between life and romance, since there was something practical in the convention. But it was not so with the pastoral; pure convention it was, and pure convention it remained during all his literary life. The real habits of shepherds were so different that they did not impinge on the eclogue.

But by being completely alien to reality, the pastoral romance seemed to elude the tyranny of facts. Everything in such a novel must be the creation of an artist, unembarrassed by memory or observation. He had unfettered liberty as to plot and episodes, remembering only that *per troppo variar Natura è bella*. It was for him to polish his periods and adorn them with verses, variable in theme and metre. By satisfying the rules of good taste he would add pleasure to an edifying picture, and the story would be *razonable* (probably something a little different from 'reasonable') if the theme were properly maintained and some philosophy injected into a context marked by elegance and decorum. The book would abide comparison with recognized masterpieces; its author's discreet invention praised, and his literary rank assigned with the general approval of persons of cultivated taste.

The standard of attainment had been set by Jorge de Montemayor's *Diana*, which had enjoyed an immense success. The *Arcadia* of Sannazaro lay behind the *Diana*, and was commended by Garcilaso's imitations. There were also other works to hand: Gil Polo's *Diana*, Lofraso's *Ten Books of Fortune*, Gálvez de Montalvo's *Pastor de Filida*. The share of each of these books in Cervantes' *Galatea* has been studied by others,[1] and it suffices here to note the supreme importance of Montemayor's book. This direct rivalry and the disappointment that ensued probably explain the harsh treatment of the Portuguese novelist in *Don Quixote*, i. 6.

By the exercise of great ingenuity critics have identified most of the characters of the novel. Elicio and Galatea are Cervantes and Catalina de Palacios in the days of their courtship. Lauso and Silena might be Barahona de Soto and an unknown, or possibly Cervantes and the troublesome Ana de Rojas, mother of his Isabel. Lauso appears in *The House of Jealousy* in the role of the poor, gifted wooer, which Cervantes had probably good reason to embody. The great shepherds Astraliano and Meliso are indubitably Don John of Austria and Don Diego Hurtado de Mendoza, and the use of some of Francisco de Figueroa's verses serves to identify Tirsi. By similiar inferences we catch glimpses of Mateo Vásquez, Cristóbal de Virués, Rey de Artieda, Gálvez de Montalvo, Gregorio

[1] See the preface to Schevill and Bonilla's edition of *La Galatea*.

Silvestre, and others. But all this labour is to no profit. The novel is not a *roman à clef*, and when we decipher the names we learn nothing whatsoever about the action.

It is more relevant to notice that the figures represent qualities. These qualities are conventional erotic attitudes inferred from the verses, but they contain the possibilities (as we shall see) of something more striking. Elicio is poor and talented, while Ergasto is honest and rough; Galatea is unequalled, Silerio is pitiable, Lenio is out of love. It is the same elsewhere. Grisóstomo is desperate, and Marcela is indifferent; Basilio is poor and talented, and Camacho is a rich boor; Rústico is a dunderhead, and Clori has an eye on the main chance. There is a kind of moral behind such attitudes, and the fact is to be noted when dealing with so exemplary a novelist.

Not all of the *Galatea* is pastoral romance. In the first book there is a short and crude drama of violence from the south of Spain, and the second and fifth books develop an exemplary novel which might have been entitled *The two Friends*. To these we must recur. On the other hand, the pastoral convention is not limited to the *Galatea* or to the promise of a second part. The sub-plot of *The House of Jealousy* is a pastoral triangle between Lauso, Rústico, and Clori, and it is possible that the ballad of *Jealousy* may have been designed to occupy a pastoral frame. Among Porcia's many disguises in *Love's Labyrinth* is the pastoral. She is found wandering, sheepless, in a sheepskin coat obviously taken from a stage wardrobe. The story of *Grisóstomo*

and Marcela is a pastoral novelette, and it is preceded by an anecdote of Antonio and Olalla. *Fair
Leandra* (*Don Quixote*, i. 51) is rather an anecdote
than a short story. *Camacho's Wedding* (*Don Quixote*,
ii. 19–21) is a rehandling of the story of Rústico,
Lauso, and Clori, but made reasonable. Camacho's
rustic opulence is quite a possible Spanish picture,
and there was doubtless precedent for Quiteria's
desertion of her true love Basilio. What is less
pardonable is the latter's Italianate trick of pretending to die, and the betrothal *in articulo mortis*.

The part taken by Don Quixote and Sancho
Panza in these adventures acutely raises their significance for Cervantes' art. They are spectators only
in the incidents of the First Part, for it would
seem that their author believed the pastoral interest
would redeem the monotony of adventures based
on real life. But in *Camacho's Wedding*, not only has
he made a strenuous effort to assimilate the pastoral
landscape to the real Spain of his hero's movements,
but he uses it to bring out an amusing opposition
of their temperaments. As the Second Part progresses the pastoral element grows. In the 58th
chapter the hero encounters a group of young
ladies and gentlemen who have studied eclogues by
Garcilaso and Camões, the latter in Portuguese, and
have taken to the fields to play them. Passing the
same spot on his return from Barcelona, in the 67th
chapter, Don Quixote plans his own Arcadia, with
all the characters of his history allotted new parts.
There is a slight difficulty about the priest, since
it is hardly seemly that he should have a shepherdess
even if he turn shepherd. By this time the mind of

Sancho had grasped the idea, and had allocated a novel part to his wife as the fat lady of the company. He stirred up the Bachelor Sansón Carrasco to compose an eclogue for their exercise; and his last appeal to his master—a superb jumble of faithful affection and muddled ideas—is pastoral:

'Ay! (Sancho answered in tears) Don't you die, sir. Take my counsel, live long. The silliest thing a man can do in this life is to let himself die, without being killed by anyone or polished off by any hands but those of his own melancholy. Don't be lazy; get up from your bed, and let's go to the field dressed as shepherds, as we have already agreed to do.' (ii. 74.)

To return to the *Galatea*, despite its author's attempts to conceal the unpleasant fact, the book was a failure or, at best, a merely reputable performance. It 'promises much and performs little' Cervantes said. The thin trickle of incident does not attract our attention, and the whole merit of the book lies in the surface style. But as an exercise in style it was of consummate importance for Cervantes. He speaks in the prologue of his desire to 'communicate the talent I have received from heaven'. The book was held back long enough to escape the charge of rashness, and issued to avoid that of niggardliness. He offered to his compatriots advantages that were 'more than mediocre'. It was not only that he had mingled instructive disquisitions from Leone Ebreo with the talk of his pseudo-shepherds, as he was entitled to do in view of their disguise; but he provided a new liberty of invention and communication.

'It cannot be denied [he wrote] that the studies of this

faculty (of letters), so highly esteemed in times past, involve more than mediocre advantages: such as the poet's enrichment in the matter of language and his dominion of the art of eloquence possible to it, for the sake of loftier and more important undertakings. He may open a road so that lesser spirits, who would like to keep the abundance of the Castilian tongue within the narrow range of an obsolete style, should come to know by his example that an open, fertile and spacious field lies before them. With ease and sweetness, gravity and eloquence, they may range freely over it, revealing the diversity of notions—acute, grave, subtle and lofty—which the favourable influence of heaven has so advantageously and universally produced in fertile Spanish minds, and every moment continues to produce in our own happy day.'

This was no hollow boast but an urgent need of the hour. At about the same time Luis de León was forced to defend the use of the vernacular for his *Names of Christ*, and Fernando de Herrera was devising a new lexicon worthy of art by his adaptations from Latin and Italian sources. The medieval rhetorician had distinguished three styles : high, middle, and low. The high style was that of the Latinists, whether ancient or modern, and it was regarded as unapproachable. The vernacular could only be exercised in the middle or low manner, according as it obeyed precepts or ignored them. For theology, philosophy, and other grave subjects the vernacular was deemed wholly unsuited, and even for literature it could not rise above the rank of a pastime. It was against this dead weight of scholastic tradition that the great writers of the sixteenth century reacted, by annexing to the vernacular those qualities of dignity, flexibility, clarity, &c., which each in his different way saw in the great Augustan writers. It is what Cervantes proposed to do in the *Galatea*, not necessarily for its own sake, but as a preparation for higher tasks.

It is for this purpose that he applies the 'colours of rhetoric' which he had learned from Dr. López de Hoyos, in all the gamut of *imitatio*, *inventio*, *amplificatio*, *distributio*, *eloquium*, and the rest. The preceptors placed imitation among the virtues, provided it was not slavish. Models existed, and the first duty of the young writer was to imitate them, and also to imitate life through them. Cervantes holds before his eyes the laudable example of Montemayor, representing all of the Vergilian eclogue that was possible within the limits of Spanish taste; but his object is to outdo the model. He concerns himself with the invention of variable incidents and characters, remembering that 'Nature is only fair through constant change'. There is an uninterrupted flow of narrative throughout the book, and we are never left too long in any one company. The experience would be exhilarating if we had any interest in his persons and scenes. In the matter of diction, the *Galatea* perfects the Cervantine period, the rotund idiom of Don Quixote. It is true that the content fails to charm, and that there were secrets of style still unrevealed. Speech was still a matter of monologues, and there was no raciness of Sevillan idiom. Sancho's language was still unborn; but Cervantes had formed for himself an eloquent phrase which had the ease of the *Diana* and the courtliness of *Amadis*, itself the lineal descendant of the *Lancelots* and *Tristans* of the French middle ages.

Ease, sweetness, gravity, and eloquence were the qualities desired. The second pair warred against the first, and the genius of the writer consisted in reconciling their quarrel. For the sake of gravity and eloquence the sentence is long, the principal verb is withheld, and an abundance of participial and concessive clauses intervene, each with its own recognizable structure. Epithets abound; they are not individually striking, but they give warmth to the phrase by spreading over it an emotional veil. We do not stop to consider their individual propriety (such halts would not be conducive to ease), but we are aware of a general enrichment. The defects of Cervantine verses have their value in his prose, since their fault was to be eloquently prosy. His use of echoes (or ' varied repetition ') belongs to an altisonant, unpoetical style. The obvious epithet and facile antithesis are easy, eloquent, and perhaps sweet. So we get such phrases as ' here he made an end of talk and a beginning of tears ' (copied from Montemayor) and ' Timbrio's tearful, the priest's moving, words '. A story is ' long to tell you, but short to weary me '. The echoes, of course, belong to his own language and can rarely be caught in another, but we can appreciate the amplification of ' hardly had the white Aurora left the tedious bed of her jealous husband ', and the use of obvious epithets in ' entering into holy temples and putting accursed hands on the sacred relics '. To attempt some kind of summary effect: ' Moors spared no-body ' becomes in the Cervantine idiom:

' Of little avail to the priest was his sanctity, to the friar his retreat, snowy locks to the aged man or gallant youth to the young, or to the child his simple innocence; all were ravaged by those miscreant dogs who, having burned the houses, robbed the temples, deflowered the virgins, killed the defenders, being yet more weary with their feat than content, returned quite unhindered at the moment when dawn came to their vessels, which were already laden with the best of the village property, the township being left desolate and unpeopled (for they had swept away most of the inhabitants, while others had in the mountains sought refuge).'

The sixth book is given over to the praise of poesy. An elaborate funeral is staged for the shepherd Meliso, whom we readily see to have been the statesman-poet Don Diego Hurtado de Mendoza. The rites are pagan and pseudo-antique, like those used for Grisóstomo in *Don Quixote*; and the treatment being entirely decorative, the panegyric of Hurtado de Mendoza does not attain to the height of the few impassioned lines on Garcilaso in *Persiles*, iii. 8. Cervantes mentions this poet in the preliminaries of the affair, together with Boscán, Castillejo, Torres Naharro, Francisco de Aldana, and Fernando de Acuña; an unequal company, interesting only as a pointer to his taste and poetical education. The Muse Calliope descends to grace the ceremony, and pronounces a lengthy verse-catalogue of living Spanish poets. Ninety-seven are listed, and the list includes only those of 'heavenly' renown. At a later date Cervantes considered that some names might have been entered without sufficient foundation; but the process of revision gave him 150 great poets for his *Voyage to Parnassus* in 1614. Annotators have found delight in these lists which, while fixing a few facts concerning the writers of the epoch, allow for indefinite commentary to supply the vacuity of Cervantes' phrases. The contemporary aims satisfied were perhaps two : Cervantes, by 'imitating' Gil Polo's *Song of the Turia*, may have hoped to achieve credit with the critics, for who could deny that a catalogue for all Spain was superior to a regional list ? Besides, he might placate the *genus irritabile vatum*. Furthermore, *Calliope's Song* was a conclusive answer to those Italians and other foreigners who continued to deny that Spain had culture. It was one more document *de asserenda Hispanorum eruditione*. The weight of numbers must bear down all opposition.

The *Voyage to Parnassus* is, in one sense, a revision of *Calliope's Song*. The list has been purged and augmented, and even a middle class of writers is indicated. Only one bad poet is mentioned, Arbolanche, author of the *Habidas* (1566), but Cervantes gives us to understand that they greatly outnumbered the good. Antonio de Lofraso, author of *The ten Books of Fortune*, is named as representative of those who have gone from good to worse. In withdrawing the favourable treatment accorded in the Scrutiny of the Books (*Don Quixote*, i. 6), Cervantes has doubtless been influenced by some personal considerations ; others appear in his complaint against the brothers Argensola, who had not elected him a member of the literary retinue of the Count of Lemos when this magnate and Maecenas travelled to his viceroyalty of Naples. To show what he might have done as an official bard, Cervantes intercalated an account of the festival of

13 May 1612 from the account by Oquina which had been licensed at Madrid on 31 August of that year. The dates serve to mark the period in which the *Voyage* was composed, but the episode is to the detriment of the work.

On the other hand, this poem was written by the man who had composed *Don Quixote* and the *Exemplary Novels*, that is to say, with the greatest narrative exuberance. The prefatory acknowledgement to Cesare Caporali's *Viaggio* is courteous to the point of superfluity, for Cervantes owes nothing of importance to Caporali. The tableau of an attack by bad poets upon Apollo and the good had been used before Cervantes in a limited way, and came to be a favourite with the eighteenth century. The theme is bookish and can never have a wide appeal; it requires dexterity, brevity, and happy phrasing. It is also naturally prosaic; Cervantes employed verse in tercets which deprived him of his best literary asset for the duration of this book, and he only recovered his true powers in the prose of the *Addendum*. His exuberant fancy betrayed him into *longueurs*; for however ingenious may be such passages as the description of Mercury's ship (all made of verses) and the various routes taken to Parnassus by the Spanish poets, they exceed the patience with which we are willing to receive this artificial theme. It is the same with his allegory of Vain Glory, Adulation, and Lying in the sixth book. Ingeniously decorative as it is, like those of the second book of *Persiles*, it adds nothing to our understanding of the causes of literary vices. On the other hand, there are passages of great interest, such as the farewell to Madrid and the dialogue between Cervantes and Apollo on the former's want of success in poetry, which are as poignant or realistic as his verse permits. The Count of Lemos' triumph in Naples is an unwelcome irrelevance, and the whole work is one in which the half would have been better than the whole.

A WRONG TURNING

Lope de Vega se alzó con la monarquía cómica.

For twenty-five years Cervantes struggled down a road which was as inevitably attractive to all men of genius as it was slippery for him. He was resolved to be a dramatic poet. He had enjoyed theatricals from the year in his boyhood when he had stared open-mouthed at the versatile Lope de Rueda. The bustling atmosphere of the back stage and the travelling company equally delighted him, for stage-folk turned the stuff of life into ingenious fantasy. Without a patron the rewards of 'straight' literature were meagre, and no one had yet made a living by his pen. To put one's name to a comedy was still unfashionable, but plays were already a source of pocket-money to ingenious young men. The creation of fixed theatres in Madrid had created a demand for new scripts, and as a proportion of the takings were used for charity, the new industry had a strong backing. The fixed stage had led to stabilization of technique, with the result that new methods clamoured for new creations.

Against this we must set the limitations of Cervantes' genius which unfitted him for success in this genre. His mind was that of a novelist, and like Lope de Vega he saw no essential difference between a play and a short story. If his rival was unsuccessful in the novel on this account, Cervantes could not master the art of drama. He failed to perceive the need for concision and unification in the ordering of his plots, and he was feeble in his curtains. He fills plays with plots and sub-plots as if he were winding through the intricacies of a prose narrative. His individual scenes are, at times, of unapproached realism, and he even wrote one whole act with plenary inspiration; but his work is full of *longueurs*. The technique which he inherited was still somewhat naïve, and he came too soon to learn any important lesson from the new art of Lope de Vega. The convention which favoured the use of verse in the theatre must have appealed powerfully to this lover of the Muses, but he lacked the lyrical gift. In *The happy Ruffian* and two interludes he was able to draw upon his rich and racy lexicon of vulgar speech, so that the economy of the lines leaves nothing to be desired ; but even such verse is not equal to the Protean Cervantine prose of the best interludes. In the latter, indeed, his success was unqualified. He proved to be the immediate heir of his admired Lope de Rueda, the perfecter of the 'little genre', and the superior of all the vast company who have followed him.

Not only in Madrid, but also in Sevilla and Valencia the new permanency of the theatre had begun to influence technique. In the days of Lope de Rueda, about the years 1560–5, the stage consisted of four planks laid across benches, a blanket for a back-cloth, some hidden singers, and three or four types with a sackful of clothes. At Toledo a certain Navarro had introduced simple effects, but the conditions were rudimentary. The plays were likely to be eclogues consisting of a loose string of scenes, and there were some adaptations from the contemporary Italian stage which showed a somewhat more serious intention. Between the scenes of the plot (such as it was) there were inserted irrelevant skits which gave an opening for the actor who could play the heavy father, braggart soldier, dunderhead, &c. So things had been when Cervantes fled to Italy, but when he returned from his Algerian captivity a dozen years later, a new technique was in vogue. Verse had driven prose from the boards, and it was customary to mingle the metres, though without any consistent principle. Four acts had come to be normal, and the whole performance included a lyrical prologue, farces delivered as interludes between the acts, and a final dance. Lope de Vega himself had composed four-act plays in his youth, but he soon produced the more workmanlike three-act type. Cervantes rewrote many of his early efforts in this manner, but he never understood it fully, and his new groupings of scenes have, at times, no significance. In place of the simple eclogue and sentimental drama of passion there had come themes of national history, rephrased ballads, plays of intrigue, and classical tragedy; and the *personae* included not only human actors, but allegorical and monstrous inventions. These things were, it seems, already common form and their invention could not clearly be ascribed to individuals. In 1615 Cervantes claimed the credit for reducing the drama from five acts to three, and for having placed moral figures on the stage by embodying the hidden imaginings and thoughts of the soul. But the Sevillan Juan de la Cueva[1] makes

[1] In the *Exemplar Poético* (1606):
> For of five acts one act I took away,
> and to *jornadas* I reduced the plot,
> setting the fashion for the present day.

a similar claim to have reduced the number of acts, and his plays abound in moral figures; and he and Cervantes studiously ignore one another.

Juan de la Cueva's plays were published in 1579, while Cervantes was still a prisoner in Africa, and his priority is indisputable. That Cervantes used his book seems to be established by the rhetoric of the *Numantia* and *Traffic of Algiers* and the way in which the verse is handled. But his rival did his work for the theatres of Sevilla, whereas Cervantes worked in Madrid, and he may not have known his plays from the first. Juan de la Cueva was not himself an original genius, for there were others to claim credit for these innovations. When Cervantes entered the field they were both common property and yet of such recent date that each new adept had some of the joys of novelty. The history of the drama which Cervantes gave in the prologue to his *Eight Comedies* may or may not have been penned in malice—we know that Juan de la Cueva had a genius for rancour—but he certainly omitted to describe the state of the theatre as he found it or name the author most typical of this style.

The division of plays into five acts was recommended and practised by the famous Torres Naharro in his *Propalladia* of 1519, and he also presented comedies of manners and romantic adventure conducted by types which were later to become commonplace. During many years his principles were ignored in Spain, but in the seventies of the sixteenth century they may have served to advance the new 'Senecan' tendencies. A five-act dramatic poem of great beauty was the *Inez de Castro* of the Portuguese professor António Ferreira. The theme was the most moving in the national annals, and at Coimbra the professor-poet could count on an audience educated both in classical principles and modern elegance. Translated and mangled by the Salamancan teacher Jerónimo Bermúdez as the *Pitiful Nise* of 1577, this poem, though shorn of its simple splendour, exerted a wide influence in Spain. It was evidence that modern drama need not hold to the low level of the farce and the eclogue, and a number of influential poets sought to emulate this achievement. In the eighties we encounter the Senecan outburst of tragedies by Lupercio Leonardo de Argensola and the two Lepantine veterans, Andrés Rey de Artieda and Cristóbal de Virués, so highly esteemed by Cervantes, in which the number of acts varies from five to three. But what gives authenticity to Juan de la Cueva's claim is that his reduction was made from the five acts employed by the Senecans of Sevilla: Guevara, Gutierre de Cetina, Cózar, Fuentes, Ortiz, Mejía, and Malara, the 'Andalusian Menander'. Represented by no surviving work, these humanists and poets are known to have written a large number of plays, and could reasonably be deemed a 'school'. In opposition to them Juan de la Cueva developed his own four-act technique, which is to be found also in the *Numantia* and *Traffic of Algiers* of Cervantes and in very early pieces by Lope de Vega. The further reduction from four to three acts, which Cervantes claims to have effected by his *Naval Battle* (about 1585), was less symptomatic of revolt against a classical norm than a step towards the new modern norm of Lope de Vega. A three-act play was extant as early as 1535, and even in a limited sense Cervantes' claim is improbable. He was not temperamentally fitted to contribute to dramatic technique.

Cervantes' plays survive from two epochs: the manuscripts of *Numantia* and *The Traffic of Algiers* represent the form in which they were presented at Madrid at some date between 1580 and 1587, but the remaining plays were issued together in 1615. They are all in three acts, and conform more or less to the precepts of Lope de Vega's 'new' comedy; but the conformity is imperfect in all cases, and in some is no more than apparent. In the famous discussion of the drama in *Don Quixote* (i. 48) Cervantes showed himself still an opponent of the 'new' comedy, which, indeed, he had hardly enjoyed leisure to know. The new style belonged to the capital, Madrid, and the Sevillan traditions known to Cervantes were both robust and more archaic. They were part of his settled technique, with the result that, even while admitting the victory of Lope de Vega in the *Eight Comedies*, he did not go beyond a superficial revision of his own manuscripts. These last plays, therefore, also comply with an older technique, and are of much earlier vintage. Some must have been contemporaries of the *Numantia* and *Traffic of Algiers*. Others, such as *The Bagnios of Algiers*, probably belong to those which he had in mind in 1592 when he offered Rodrigo Osorio, of Sevilla, six plays on the understanding that they were not to be paid for unless admittedly the best ever put on the Spanish stage.

It was on 5 March 1585 that Cervantes con-

tracted with Gaspar de Porras to supply two plays—
The confused Comedy and *The Traffic of Constantinople
with Selim's Death*—for twenty ducats. The former
was certainly written, because Cervantes reckoned
it the best in his repertory. Both in the *Voyage to
Parnassus* (iv) and in the *Addendum* he praises his
work, claiming that it would rank high among the
best comedies of contemporary life. The words
'confused' and 'confusion' are leitmotifs of the
extant *Love's Labyrinth*, a most confused play, and
there can be little doubt that this is the same piece,
with no more than superficial modifications. It
carries to an extreme Cervantes' delight in inventiveness. The existence of the play under another
name helps us to make other identifications. Our
author claimed to have put successfully on the
boards twenty or thirty plays during his early residence in Madrid (1580–7), though we cannot be
certain whether the figure is to be accepted. He
offered six to Osorio in 1592, and they may already
have been written, and significantly it is still six
that he mentions as ready for the press in the *Addendum to the Parnassus*. Next year he published eight,
but that is no evidence that two were new plays;
on the contrary, the latest was *Pedro de Urdemalas*,
assignable on internal evidence to 1610 or 1611.

The House of Jealousy and Woods of the Ardenne
must be the same as the *Enamoured Wood* of the
early Madrid period. The division into three acts
sits very loosely on the play, which is connected
with the *Galatea* by its pastoral sub-plot exploiting
the same notion of merit versus wealth; it is linked
to the *Numantia* by its elaborate use of phantoms and

allegorical figures and by its stiff versification. *The Grand Turkess* can hardly be other than the surviving *Grand Sultana*, in which the character of Madrigal is a duplicate of the teasing sacristan of the Algerine plays. In this case, however, the marks of revision are clear. Catalina de Oviedo is said to have been sent to Constantinople about 1600 and to have been kept six years in the harem concealed from the Grand Turk. The date is given in a ballad which Cervantes offers as the ostensible authority for his play, and its occurrence in rhyme provokes suspicion. The lady's name seems designed to rhyme with *divina* and *peregrina*, and as there was no historical Catalina de Oviedo remotely resembling in authority Cervantes' heroine, we must treat all these indications with distrust. There was a Çuffija, daughter of a governor of Corfu, in the harem of Sultan Murad, who wielded great power for twenty-eight years, and Ukrainian ballads praise Marusia Bogoslavka, the counterpart of the historical Roxolana. A mention of the Persian embassy to Spain in 1599 contains no reference to the return visit of 1613. The history of this play would seem to be long and complex. It must have been presented, if we are to credit Cervantes' own words, at Madrid before 1587. There may have been a revision undertaken at Sevilla in or after 1599, and the existing form must date from 1607 or later.

Other dates are more approximately determined, and some of them show how these comedies intertwine with the *Exemplary Novels* and *Don Quixote*. In length and plot there is not much to choose between a comedy and an exemplary novel, the difference lying in the suitability of the genre for Cervantes' genius. *The gallant Spaniard* is a dramatization of a feat by a certain Maldonado at Castelnovo in Dalmatia. The issue was whether discipline cancelled the demands of military honour. Maldonado, forbidden to leave his post to fight a duel, clambered over the walls and met his challenger. His case was discussed and his action vindicated in Don Gerónimo Ximénez de Urrea's *Dialogue of true military Honour* (1566). There is nothing else to indicate when this play was written, though Cervantes would acquire his knowledge of Oran at first hand in 1581, when he visited that city on a mission from Philip II. The experience of captivity suggested to him, as we have seen, the two motifs of 'the crossed lovers' and 'the captive captain', giving the chain: *The Traffic of Algiers, The liberal Lover, The Bagnios of Algiers, The History of the captive Captain* (*Don Quixote*, i. 39–42). The relative order is fixed by the way in which the motives succeed one another, and in the last case by the presence of letters in a revised form, and the whole were extant by the middle of 1604. It would appear, therefore, that *The Bagnios* must have been executed at Sevilla, possibly as part of the project of 1592. *The happy Ruffian* is based on Fr. Agustín Dávila Padilla's history of the Dominican province of St. James, which was published at Madrid in 1596. The first act shows an intimate knowledge of Sevilla and the life of its ruffians such as we know he had opportunities to acquire between 1596 and the end of the century, the hey-day of such polished rogues as Antonio Álvarez de Soria. This was probably the

date of the first act, if not of the whole play. At
the beginning of the second act Cervantes justifies
his disregard of the unities of time and place, despite his insistence on such in *Don Quixote* (i. 48),
at least in so far as they affect verisimilitude. This
play corresponds in tone to the exemplary novel of
Rinconete and Cortadillo (written before 1604) and
the interlude of *The widowed Ruffian. The Comedy
of Entertainment* treats the theme of Cardenio's
timidity in a manner different from the sub-plot of
Don Quixote, i. It is a revision of the earlier conception, since Cervantes makes more flagrant the
psychological weakness of Cardenio, and he exacts
a severer penalty. An allusion to a nunnery in
Cantillanas Street could not be satisfied before
1609, and the interest shown in astrology resembles
that of *The Dogs' Colloquy* and *Persiles*, i, which both
probably date from that year. The best of the play
belongs to the servants, and Cristinica the kitchen-
maid is a twin of the Cristinica of *The careful Guard*
(1611). Finally, the use of the gipsy motif in *Pedro
de Urdemalas* is intermediate between the first hint
in *The Dogs' Colloquy* (1609) and the full bloom in
The little Gipsy. An allusion to the actor Nicolás el
Romo (d. 20 March 1610), as if still alive, seems
to fix the date with precision.

From these dates it becomes clear that Cervantes'
dramas represent a persistent effort spread over a
quarter of a century to conquer the esteem of the
theatre-going public. Failure to please and, no
doubt, his disorderly methods of composition caused
gaps in the activity, but did not suspend it. The
end came only when he had resolved, under pain of

hunger, to sell his scripts for what they would fetch, and even then he was occupied with *The optical Illusion*, 'which (if I do not delude myself) is sure to give contentment'. The fee was a moderate one, but it was obtained without wrangling with actors. But though a continuous effort, the comedies have to be discussed in two divisions owing to the suspicion which necessarily attaches to those published in 1615. The suspicion may be mostly groundless, for even the most obvious difference between the older and later comedies—the change from four acts to three—took place during the early Madrid years in respect of the lost *Naval Battle*.

The two early plays are remarkable. The *Numantia* is perhaps the boldest expression in literature of desperate Spanish patriotism: that reckless, undisciplined, unyielding devotion seen at Zaragoza during the Napoleonic invasion, and in the defences of the Alcázar of Toledo and of Madrid by the combatants of the recent Civil War. The inspiration is far superior to the execution, which is crude and vacillating. Inferior motives are exploited in the plot, which is a disorderly mass of scenes embodying imperfectly related histories; and the characters are of the most wooden uniformity. The Romans are so entirely 'Roman' that the first act is largely wasted on their mutual admiration as examples of Roman virtue. It is true that the theme is the restoration of military discipline, but nothing less than the highest conduct appears on the stage. The Numantines—with Greek and modern Italianate names—are even nobler than the Romans. In the contest of virtue, by dying to the last man, they rob Scipio of the triumph he had earned. This final scene, however, is given to a boy who enters the play for the first time in the last act, and it is not connected with the leading Numantine figures. The latter rush successively on to the stage at the end for no better purpose than to utter heroic speeches and leave their corpses in the public view. There is the same disproportion between the intention and the effect of the supernatural element. Cervantes wishes to view the defence of Numantia *sub specie aeternitatis*, and for this purpose Spain and the Duero enter into a dialogue (to prophesy the sack of Rome by Spanish troops in 1517), and War, Disease, and Famine discuss the crisis of the action. There is a certain stiff dignity in the dialogue which, in its altisonant verses, might have figured in a neo-classical heroic epic. For the tragic emotion, however, Cervantes is inclined, like all Spanish heroic poets since Lucan, to substitute horror; and the scenes of incantation, though intended to represent historical verisimilitude, verge on the disgusting. The incredible perfection of Roman and Numantine virtue, incantations, and severe adherence to his sources (especially Diego de Valera's abbreviated chronicle of Spain and a ballad in Timoneda's *Rosa gentil*), are signs of his lofty respect for the drama as art. This is his only tragedy, whether in prose or verse.

The intervention of mythical figures recalls his boast to have been the first to represent the imaginings and hidden thoughts of the soul. A witch calls up a devil in *The Traffic of Algiers*, and Aurelio is there tempted by Occasion and Need. In the early

House of Jealousy we encounter Venus, Cupid, Castile, Merlin, Fear, Suspicion, Despair, Curiosity, Jealousy, Ill Fame, Good Fame, and the Spirit of Paris. A conversation between Comedy and Curiosity prefaces the second act of *The happy Ruffian*, but it does not affect the action. The practice was dropped on revision, as in *The Bagnios of Algiers*. It is so general in Juan de la Cueva that Cervantes' claim to originality must be dismissed out of hand.

If the *Numantia* tends to break into unrelated scenes, this is yet more true of *The Traffic of Algiers*, in which there are individual scenes of the raciest vivacity. A kind of plot concerning the tangled affections of Aurelio and Silvia is designed to hold the play together, but it can never have excited more than a languid interest. The motive of the 'crossed lovers' is good in itself, but the exposition is intermittent and lacks breadth of character or incident. But there is a scene of the break-up of a Spanish family in the slave market of Algiers which is unequalled in Spanish dramatic literature for truth and vigour; another gives a platform for the soldier Saavedra passionately to address Philip of Spain, and in another he distinguishes between the uncompromising and the temporizing Christian; we see the insolence of a young apostate—precisely the younger of two boys in the enslaved family; there is a harrowing narrative of an attempt to escape to Oran, and invincible courage in the recaptured slave; a martyrdom is recounted with simple courage. Taken individually, these scenes had power to save the 'new' comedy from its too ready acceptance of slick conventions. Spanish drama of the classical period, had it possessed the self-respect of Cervantes' workmanship, might have stood beside Shakespeare's for profundity and truth. It was unfortunate that Cervantes did not possess the technical skill to make his meaning clear.

In *The Bagnios* this strength becomes weakness. There is, it is true, an effective opening describing a raid on the Valencian sea-shore, but elsewhere we note the dead hand of convention. The use of a double plot merely divides the interest. The bitter reality of apostasy was removed in order to insert a sugary scene of boy martyrdom modelled on the history of St. Justus and St. Pastor. With *The gallant Spaniard* we encounter a play which, though based on Algerine experience, shows a new technique. Its plot progresses regularly, and its motive is ethical. Had it been written in prose it would have made an excellent novelette; but in verse and as a play, though less incoherent than the rest, it falls short of its due effect. As for *The House of Jealousy*, it cannot have been much improved by revision. The source is Boiardo, modified by Ariosto. Angelica appears at Charlemagne's court in order to sow strife between the paladins and lure them into disastrous battle against her enchanted brother. She is so successful that Roland and Reynald rush on and off the stage with bewildering alternation, and Angelica is scarcely less fleet of foot. An ineffective magician, Malgesí, merely augments the confusion; and for patriotic reasons Bernardo del Carpio is represented as a spectator, until he is supernaturally recalled to the defence of Spain. In a pastoral sub-plot Clori is

courted by the clever Lauso and the rich Rústico.
Though the latter is demonstrated to be an ass by
means of some pranks, Clori, like Sancho, 'holds
to the king'. *Love's Labyrinth* (originally *The confused Comedy*) is a mere jumble of scenes, fit to
prove an inventiveness devoid of all rational bounds.
Taking for a starting-point the Aldingar or Lohengrin motif (the lady falsely accused and delivered
by an unknown, unexpected knight) Cervantes
introduced the complication that the base accuser
was her true lover, desirous (with the lady's com-
plicity) of putting off her father's plans for another
match. To accuse her of fornication and leave her
in peril of the stake was, it seems, a trifle in a
comedy. The matter is complicated by the notion
that her official fiancé would wish to investigate
the accusation before defending her honour, being
himself under suspicion of having abducted another.
This unabducted, runaway princess is merely bent
on matrimony, while her brother is also present
with the single purpose of errant adventure. Yet
another princess is stalking the brother, and for no
adequate reason she takes the place of the original
heroine at the stake. Everybody is on the stage at
the end and, when the unmasking comes, everybody
is doing the wrong thing. The confusing and laby-
rinthine character of such a plot is evident. The
first suggestion came, no doubt, from the Ginevra
episode of the *Orlando Furioso*.

It was from achievements of this sort that Cervantes came to write the famous 48th chapter of
the First Part of *Don Quixote*. Without any relevance to the main action, he expressed through the

respectable mouth of a Canon of Toledo his dissatis-
faction with the formula of the 'new' comedy. It
is unlikely that he knew it well, for the chapter
may have been drafted in Sevilla. The new formula
had been carefully elaborated between Lope de
Vega and his audiences. Without actually inventing
any of its elements, Lope had created a new dramatic
manner through studying the reactions of the public to plays by himself and other writers. Whatever
he found to succeed he embodied in fresh works.
In this way the populace, and especially the up-
roarious groundlings, could be called the arbiter of
plays, to which Lope himself denied (though with
mental reserves) the title of art. There was nothing
vulgar in the expenditure of much exquisite poetry
in these plays, of wide knowledge, and even of deep
or exact thought, but in principle, at least, the 'new'
comedy lacked self-respect. The universal love-
interest, the lack of repose, the indecorous intrusion
of farce at grave moments, the complications of the
plot, the substitution of types for characters, the
botched conclusions and careless middles, all these
were consequences of want of self-respect in the
theatrical art. Cervantes had striven in his own way
to achieve seriousness, historicity, verisimilitude,
and he felt an obscure distaste for a manner *ex pro-
fesso* vulgar and indifferent to all but success. The
Canon's criticism is partial, for it is merely inci-
dental in a work of entertainment. It is hag-ridden
with the notion of the unbending norm, and it
points to no practicable solution; but had it found
an exponent like Marlowe, it might have saved the
Spanish theatre from much triviality and indecorum.

From this position Cervantes did not diverge in later life; but he recognized the indubitable superiority of Lope de Vega's dramatic genius, and in the dialogue in *The happy Ruffian* he justified miracles and disunity of space on the basis of his documentation. He goes so far as to make Comedy say

> In modern times all things I show
> not as of old in narrative,
> but act.

The older style, like Cervantes' plays, was essentially rhetorical, with much to say and little to do. The new style required continuous action, and the demands it made on the imagination could be met by intelligent spectators. Therefore Comedy and Cervantes were satisfied, but not entirely:

> Though not convinced at every point,
> in part I'm satisfied.

This play is in a class by itself, since it reveals unmistakably a second style. The first act presents the lively figure of the genial young ruffian Cristóbal de Lugo. Like Carriazo and Avendaño he has turned roisterer out of sheer high spirits; and he takes a perverse pleasure in uttering farouche threats, beating up the police, and patronizing irregular establishments. But he has his *ne plus ultra*; when he finds himself on the brink of robbery to supply his needs, he is shocked into repentance. The figure stands out in the round, and the detailed knowledge of Sevillan roguery is in the style of *Rinconete*. The language also is strenuous and real. It would be most reasonable to suppose that this piece was composed in Sevilla in 1596 or later. The second and third acts reveal a disastrous falling off of power. They represent respectively the saintly penance and edifying death of this person, who was one of the most revered missionaries to Mexico. Cervantes justifies the change of scene by his documentation, and his rubrics repeatedly allege that the events were duly attested. The author was compelled to jog his flagging credulity, and the things he so tepidly believed he could not pass on to his readers.

The remaining plays belong to his late years in Madrid: *The Grand Sultana, The Comedy of Entertainment*, and *Pedro de Urdemalas*. The first, as we have seen, was probably a revised form of *The grand Turkess*, performed at Madrid about the year 1585, but the present draft cannot have been older than 1607 and was never acted. Cervantes sought to exploit his Algerine experiences in the more imposing milieu of Constantinople; but he knew nothing of that city, and so loses the advantage of topical truth. The main plot and a sub-plot are based on a theme very dear to Cervantes, namely, the resistance of Christians to Moslem blandishments. In the case of the buffoon Madrigal this constancy takes the form of high spirits, which urge him to play malicious tricks on the Jews and impudently to deceive the Cadi. In the case of the heroine her Christian constancy is shown in her repugnance to receive the embraces of the Grand Signor. She imposes what should have been impossible conditions—the use of her own religion, language, dress, customs, and the oblivion of his harem. But the Turk is yet more magnanimous, and by his sheer refusal to use constraint she is brought to yield thus far. Yet a third plot is about a Hungarian couple who had fallen into the seraglio, the girl as a captive and the boy in female disguise. Something of the sort appears again in *The History of the Moor Ricote* in *Don Quixote*, ii, but Cervantes does not work out the situation in the novel. In the play it degenerates into silly farce ; and it is farce that ruins what might have been a heroic play.

In *The Comedy of Entertainment*, which cannot have been written before 1609, we encounter the case of Cardenio the timid. The plot is not that of *Don Quixote*, i, but is perhaps yet more fit to reveal the weakness of the protagonist. Being introduced into Marcela's house in the false colours of her rich Peruvian cousin and fiancé, Cardenio is never able to resolve to woo her. In the end the cousin comes, and the play ends without a match. The name of Dorotea is here given not to the heroine but to an attendant. The main plot leaves the reader unsatisfied, but there is a brilliant sub-plot of life below stairs as the wench Cristinica takes her pick of lovers; and these lively people stage an interlude within the action which forms a ninth to the eight printed elsewhere in the volume. In *Pedro de Urdemalas* the interest is akin to that of *Licentiate Glass* and *The little Gipsy*. The protagonist is a typical figure like Lazarillo and Tyl Eulenspiegel, serving to unite anecdotes of shrewd pranks. His perverse ingenuity appeared under many disguises, and in this play he serves as an assessor to a provost, as gipsy, beggar, and actor. In this way his career

became a string of social criticisms not unlike those
of the novel. The connexion with *The little Gipsy*
lies in the plot: the story of the changeling Belica
and her instinctive refusal of marriage proposals.
She is recognized at last for the lost daughter of a
royal couple, whose presence overloads this play.
Belica, too, is pert and unfeeling; a good deal of
human kindness was needed to transform her into
the gentle, though sprightly, Preciosilla.

Drama is not to be judged apart from the stage,
and the fact that some of these pieces 'were recited
without offering of cucumbers or other missiles, and
ran their career without hisses, shouts or uproar'
(as Cervantes says) is no proof that they were successful. Already in the year of the Armada Lope
de Vega had become monarch of the stage, with his
slick and efficient formula; nor did Cervantes enjoy
the social prestige that made Lupercio Leonardo de
Argensola's Senecan tragedies appreciated by the
cognoscenti. He intervened at a critical moment, but
did violence to his own genius; for he lacked lyrical gift and dramatic instinct. He complicated his
themes till they were too ravelled to follow, and he
indulged in the most inopportune licence of farce.
His versification and stage conventions were of an
order virtually outmoded by the new conditions of
the fixed theatre. Nor are the plays even read with
pleasure; and yet the Cervantine achievement is
instructive. He practised before the 'love interest'
became the universal motor of comedy and tragedy,
and his range is the wider. He essayed the tragedy
of high patriotism, realistic portrayal of foreign
and home life, the kitchen and the caravan, social

comment, elegant intrigue, outstanding virtue, and romantic luxuriance. The variety displayed in so few plays is remarkable, and so is the list of his living characters : Saavedra and the apostate boy, the happy ruffian, the constant Christian, Cristinica and her court, and the timid Cardenio. In the 'new' comedy the young men and maidens are the same persons under different names. His unit of construction is the isolated scene, and of these there are many of extraordinary vivacity, and even one whole act. His failure to influence his contemporaries deprived them of some measure of artistic idealism, of self-respect as playwrights, and left them practising, with monotonous cleverness, a restricted convention.

It was his power to write dramatic scenes with the hand of a master that gave rise to Cervantes' consummate interludes, the high-water mark of the 'little theatre' in Spain. Here everything favoured his success. Only two are in verse (or three if we add the interlude in *The Comedy of Entertainment*), and this verse is of the direct, racy, and plebeian kind which he could handle so effectively. The rest are in prose as plastic as that of *Don Quixote*. Precedent required vignettes of real life, thumb-nail sketches of characters, and contemporary satire in the interludes; and no one save Velázquez had so true an eye to a living model as Cervantes. There may have been other interludes by him, such as the sombre *Prison of Sevilla*, but only those are certain which he himself published. They suffice to show how he carried to perfection the technique of Lope de Rueda, enlarging the range of dramatic observation.

He had a worthy successor in Quiñones de Bena-
vente, but not an equal. In the playlets of Don
Ramón de la Cruz Spanish drama recovered the
directness of Cervantine observation, and this 'little
theatre' has since been the palladium of the art.
Never presumptuous, it reaches at intervals its own
perfection; and at all times it serves as an invaluable
school for actors (who must hit off their type in a
few words), for the public (which compares a rapid
succession of such sketches), and for authors (who
learn the crude rudiments of their trade). Based as
they are on the dramatic scene, these interludes are
in keeping with other powerful or shrewd scenes
in Cervantes' formal comedies; and there is not,
despite appearances, any reason for contrasting the
successful writer of skits with the unhappy author
of comedies.

The interludes belong to the fifties and sixties of
his life, when he had attained his full stature. *The
widowed Ruffian*, *The jealous old Man*, and *The Election of the Provosts of Daganzo* go back to his period
of residence in Sevilla either in theme or style. The
first is a cynical, yet sympathetic, portrait of the
rogue Trampagos who has just lost his inamorata.
It shows him romanticizing his loss and striving to
be dull, then accepting consolation, and at last
making a roistering election between two new can-
didates for the honour. The title recalls that of
The happy Ruffian, and the two hoydens are twin
sisters of Cariharta and La Gananciosa in *Rinconete*,
while the verse has the incisive vulgarity of the
invective against Medina Sidonia. The second of
the group is simply *The jealous Extremaduran* related

without moral intent. By his insensate jealousy the
old man irritates his young wife into infidelity, and
the fun lies in the guile used on her behalf. The
point at issue in the case of the provosts is the need
for education in the public service. The same idea
occurs in the first act of *Pedro de Urdemalas* and is
given eternal youth in the famous counsels to Sancho
Panza. The play and the interlude are especially
alike in the ridicule they pour on country bumpkins
in office. As this interlude is in verse it was probably
quite an early work. *The Miracle Show* is another
satire on presumptuous rustics. It is a variant of
'the Emperor's new clothes'; there is actually no
show, but no one dares to say so since the exhibitor
has declared it to be visible only to those of pure
conscience.

The Divorce Court Judge and *The careful Guard* put
on the stage a soldier who may well be Cervantes
himself. In the first case the soldier speaks of the
tedium of marriage, and in the second, unable to
make more than a pittance out of gentlemanly commissions, the soldier is outbid by a mere sacristan.
Apart from this possible personal interest there is
a rich and tolerant humanism in *The Divorce Court
Judge* which might cause it to rank highest among
these petty dramas. Its companion and *The sham
Biscayan* are of the year 1611, which would also suit
The Cave of Salamanca, one of Cervantes' discerning
studies of student knavery. It is a quality which
he accepts and represents for itself, without moral
afterthought, and therefore serves as a reminder
that his instinct for truth was deeper than the literary principle which required him to mix the useful

with the sweet. It is not surprising, therefore, that even in the *Exemplary Novels* his eye sometimes strays from the moral (which theoretically justifies the story) to the living tableau.

LABORATORY

Yo soy el primero que he novelado en lengua castellana.

THE years which Cervantes devoted to the drama beheld also the growth of his powers as an exemplary novelist. A volume was issued under that title in 1613, but several of its items had been written many years previously, and there were others not included within its covers. These short stories link the *Galatea* of 1585 to the *Persiles* of 1617, and out of them sprang *Don Quixote*. Arising at intervals alongside the Cervantine comedies, they exploit the same motifs in many cases and have the same dimensions; they show similar phases of development. In the claim to have been the first writer of *novelle* in Spain Cervantes epitomized his contribution to literature; for out of the laboratory of the *novelle* or short stories came the first and best of novels.

The word 'novel' signified for Cervantes and his contemporaries the short story only, and for the more elaborate sort of narrative he had no more distinctive word than 'history'. By the word 'exemplary' it has been doubted whether he could have meant morally exemplary. Yet this doubt cannot stand in face of his own strenuous assertion that

'if by any means it should happen that the reading of these short stories might induce in the reader an evil desire or thought, I would rather cut off my hand than bring them before the public.'

He who had lost the use of his left hand at Lepanto would not lightly pledge his right. His examples are not, M. Paul Hazard has remarked, always *bons à suivre*; but to ask for edification only is unduly to

limit Cervantes' freedom to instruct. The Venerable
Bede, whose character is beyond attack, saw in the
examples of history not only virtues to follow but
vices to avoid. Both kinds exist among Cervantes'
stories, together with a third class more peculiarly
his own. These are the novels of 'honest recreation'.
'Honest and agreeable exercises do not hurt, but
profit', he wrote, and again: entertainers 'are as
necessary in the republic, as glades and avenues and
recreative prospects, and all things conducive to
honest recreation'. Recreation is re-creation: doing
again, so to speak, the creative work of God. The
reader's advantage may be neither from exhortation
nor from warning, but in some more diffused better-
ment. The effect, though less crudely defined, is no
less moral.

These three conceptions of the exemplary func-
tion existed in Cervantes' mind not simultaneously
but (allowing for overlapping) as three successive
phases. In the early *Liberal Lover* he displayed an
extreme of virtue, but in the middle period he un-
covers the consequences of vice. We may learn from
Rinconete and Cortadillo to what extent crime may be
organized under a slack government. It may be disconcerting to our prudery to realize that we like his
scamps and find something to admire in such honour
as is to be found among thieves; in short, that there
is actually nothing human that is alien to us. But
it was not for Cervantes to conceal the fact of vice,
nor to deny that the vicious might have engaging
qualities and act out of pure high spirits or under
the constraint of others. There is, however, in these
pieces a shifting of the centre of interest from the

moral to the picture. The picture of Monipodio's house holds our attention because it held that of its maker; and in the analysis of the effects of jealousy in *The jealous Extremaduran* we remember this unbaring of a tortured soul rather than the trite warning not to trust duennas. The third conception is exemplified in the late *Little Gipsy*. No particular moral can be drawn from the history of a lost child unexpectedly rediscovered; but the reader is honestly pleased with her frankness and self-respect, and he may be edified incidentally by Preciosilla's eloquent dissertations on the maidenly virtues.

From the catalogue we may exclude novels in the pastoral vein. In them it was essential that the shepherds should be such only in name, their habitat and occupations being unlike those of real experience. It is on those terms that we are invited to accept the philosophy of Leone Ebreo, bodily inserted into the *Galatea*. In the casuistry of love the Arcadians occupy characteristic mental positions, according as they are passionate or cynical or merely rich and vulgar; but there is hardly room for moral choice in that best of all possible worlds. The actual occurrence of the *Exemplary Novels*, however, is one of Cervantes' main planks. He uses Spanish appellatives and defines the place of action. *The Spanish Englishwoman* ended in Sevilla and was written for the private information of the archbishop, and *The little Gipsy* is a history attested by the poets of Murcia. We know from other sources that there was a thieves' kitchen in Sevilla under some semblance of discipline, and the Campuzano of *Tricked into Marriage* was a soldier known to Cervantes himself. It is true that these verifications are misleading and cover a fertile genius for invention, but they are so characteristic of the exemplary novel that we are emboldened to exclude from this class such brief pastorals as *Grisóstomo and Marcela* or *Camacho's Wedding*.

The exemplary novels are, however, a continuous development from the pastoral *Galatea*. In the first book there already occurs a brief and sanguinary tragedy of *Lisandro*, firmly located in Andalusia and not to be connected with oviculture. More conclusive is the story of Silerio and Timbrio which forms the sub-plot of the romance and occupies large tracts of the second and fifth books. This is not an affair of shepherds by the banks of the Tagus, but of young gallants who travel from Jerez to Naples and win Italian brides. They were involved with bandits in Barcelona and Algerine pirates on the sea, and part of the action took place in the year 1576, when Don John of Austria was preparing at Milan to lead an army into the Netherlands. It is a moral story, and the moral is given in the first paragraph:

'It suffices to know that, either because of his great goodness or by the force of the stars inclining me thereto, I strove by all means to become his particular friend; and heaven so favoured me that our acquaintances, almost forgetting the name of Timbrio and mine of Silerio, called us only *the two friends*, a reputation which we established by our continual intercourse and acts of friendship.'

The two Friends, for want of any other, may serve as the title of this novelette which deals with the extravagant Renaissance virtue of friendship. Out of friendship Silerio gains a hearing for Timbrio with an exalted lady, and the same motive causes him to abandon the field when he might have advanced his own suit. Timbrio requites this devotion by seeking out his friend and giving him the hand of the lady's sister. Friendship is superior to the love of the sexes, though in a well-ordered world love is added thereunto.

This story must have been completed between the internal date of 1576 and the year 1583 when the *Galatea* was ready for the press. It proposes a virtue to be imitated, and the plot is arbitrarily woven to suit the moral. It is anchored to real life by the picture of banditry in the hinterland of Barcelona and piracy on the high seas, both being excerpts from the biography of the author. There are no proper dialogues, but only alternate harangues, and the narrative is clogged by screeds of verse. Apart from a diminution of the poetical matter, these features are also to be found in *The liberal Lover*. They form a technique which may be summarized thus: positive moral intention, arbitrary plot and characterization, verisimilitude of some episodes drawn from Cervantes' Algerine days, rhetorical phrasing, use of soliloquies and harangues, lack of dialogue and of racy common speech. *The liberal Lover* proposes an example of extreme magnanimity in a lover, who does not reckon his utmost services to be a claim on his lady's goodwill. It is the case of the Grand Turk in *The Grand Sultana*, which we believe was also *The grand Turkess* of about the year 1585. The central episode represents the two enslaved lovers prosecuting their own courtship as if pleading the causes of their master and mistress;

and this theme of 'the crossed lovers' gives the principal plot of *The Traffic of Algiers*, of the early Madrid period, and one of two plots for *The Bagnios*. The action begins in 1574 and covers the Mediterranean and Aegean.

How many other novelettes are to be attributed to this first class is, in view of the difficulty of fixing their dates, hard to determine. *The History of the captive Captain* formed part of *Don Quixote*, i, from the middle of 1604, and may have been composed earlier. It uses the second plot of *The Bagnios*, together with a couple of letters in a revised form. The theme is adventurous rather than moral, but it does represent the contact of Christian and Moor without compromise of Christian principles. Its verisimilitude is autobiographical. Cervantes attached to it a romantic appendix, *The Muleteer*, showing how a youth took to this profession in order to follow his love. The action of *The Call of the Blood*, we are informed, took place before the sacrament of marriage became obligatory in Spain. If Cervantes was using more than a vague memory of a former state, this would be before 1564, when Philip II introduced the Tridentine ruling. At the supposed time of narration the heroine had become a grandmother. The indication is vague, but suggests a date before 1600. If there is a virtue exemplified, it is that of discretion in matters of honour; but discretion, with Cervantes, is a nebulous, though important, merit, and is hard to distinguish from mere inaction. By her discretion and that of her parents the heroine conceals her shame until Providence sets her to rights. Providence works through the appeal which blood-kinship inevitably makes, for the grandfather is intuitively drawn to his own grandchild. Two other studies of the point of honour are included in *Persiles*, namely *Antonio the Barbarian* and *Renato and Eusebia*. The former is said to open during the Emperor Charles V's wars against the German Protestants in 1544–6, and it closes about twenty years later. It arises from the use of a contemptuous expression by a young blood to a worthy soldier. This may have corresponded, as we have seen, to an event of Cervantes' own career in 1569, and the probability is increased by its attribution to himself idealized in the figure of Don Fernando de Saavedra, the good soldier of *The gallant Spaniard*. *Renato and Eusebia* uses the Aldingar or Lohengrin motif from the story of Ginevra in the *Orlando Furioso*, but with a difference. It supposes the champion of truth to have been beaten in fight, and to have lain under a stigma for a score of years until righted by a death-bed confession. *Love's Labyrinth* uses the same motif with a different twist and is based on *The confused Comedy* of 1585. The internal date offered by *Renato and Eusebia* is that of Charles V's retirement to Yuste. The associations of both these stories are thus early, and their technique, though modified for inclusion in the *Persiles*, is not unlike that of an exemplary novel of this first vintage.

The second vintage may be called Sevillan, not merely because some most important stories were written there, but because of the radical change in outlook and language produced by experience of Sevilla. They offer examples of vices to avoid; characters observed from life are worked out by incidents which spring from character; the preoccupation with plot is slight; language is racy, and there is keen dialogue; verisimilitude is established not by memories of the years at Algiers but by observed facts of Sevillan life.

Certain dates may be securely established for novels in this series. A manuscript prepared for the Archbishop of Sevilla by the Licentiate Porras de la Cámara in 1606 contained *Rinconete and Cortadillo*, *The jealous Extremaduran*, and *The feigned Aunt*. The last of the group was not issued with others in 1613, and its attribution to Cervantes has been contested. But if it be not his, a greater difficulty remains; for it would then have to be by a novelist equal to Cervantes, using his formula before it had been given to the public. For the Cervantine exemplary novel was not identical with anything that had preceded it. Its predecessors on the Spanish side were apologues, and on the Italian anecdotes. The anecdotal element is perceptible even in Boccaccio, who sometimes writes with Cervantine fullness. The exemplary novel was a complete history, though short and without complications. It resembled the modern single-volume novel more than the telegraphic modern short story; while Cervantes' full-dress novels correspond to modern three-deckers. To have achieved this form apart from Cervantes, and to show all the characteristics of the second epoch just enumerated, seems to postulate a deutero-Cervantes, which is impossible. *The feigned Aunt* is genuine, and was written in or before 1606. *Rinconete and Cortadillo* may be carried back as far as the middle of 1604, in view of the fact that it came out of the same valise as *The curious Impertinent*—itself unquestionably an exemplary story of this sort (*Don Quixote*, i. 47). *Tricked into Marriage* and *The Dogs' Colloquy* belong to 1609; the date being fixed partly by the allusion in the latter to the imminent expulsion of the Moriscos, and partly by the first appearance of the myth of Maldonado, the gipsy count, which is exploited more fully in *Pedro de Urdemalas* and *The little Gipsy*. Only part of *The illustrious Kitchen-wench* (of 1608 ?) belongs to this group, which includes *Licentiate Glass* (1510 ?) on two counts. These pieces show that the second period overlaps the third, which is romantic or sentimental.

From internal evidence we learn that the significant years were from 1589 to 1599. The period during which crime attained its apogee in the Andalusian metropolis is fixed at 1589 by *The Dogs' Colloquy*; for it was during the 'assistantship' of Juan Sarmiento de Valladares that Monipodio the fence and his attendant ruffians were unchecked. This was the Golden Age of Alfonso Álvarez de Soria, executed in 1603, Gonzalo Genís (executed in 1596 by order of the Count of Priego), and Ribera; the first being certainly known to Quevedo and probably to Cervantes, and the others mentioned in *The illustrious Kitchen-wench*. These considerations enable us to fix the ideal date of *Rinconete* in 1589. Cervantes records the suppression of barefaced crime by the 'assistant' Count of Puñonrostro, who policed Sevilla from 1597 to 1599. These internal dates, of course, do not fix the times when the novels were written, but they make a bracket with the evidence given in the previous paragraph. The action of *Licentiate Glass* takes place while Valladolid was capital of Spain, that is, between 1602 and 1608 ; but the unflattering references to that city were presumably written in Madrid.

The avoidance of vice is preached in several of them. At the close of *Rinconete* we learn 'how badly justice was administered in that famous city of Sevilla, since folk so pernicious and contrary to Nature itself lived almost openly in it', and *The Dogs' Colloquy* bears the same moral. In these pieces social satire predominates, taking a bookish or conventional turn in *Licentiate Glass*. *The jealous Extremaduran* survives in two forms, and has two morals. In the version of 1613 it serves as a warning against duennas, being thus a counterpart of Sancho Panza's skirmishes against the duenna Rodríguez ; but in the Porras manuscript of 1606 there is an attempt to throw on the jealous old husband the whole blame for his wife's misconduct. Esperanza ('Hope') achieved marriage at the end of *The feigned Aunt* by her beauty and discretion ; but the author reminds us that very few Hopes could entertain this hope. The aunt herself is mercilessly condemned. Modern readers have jibbed at this conclusion as immoral and unlike Cervantes. The defence of a pander in *The happy Ruffian* and the affairs of Maritornes in *Don Quixote* dispose of the allegation that the treatment is unlike Cervantes ; and the fact that he could see a victim in a sinner represents an advance in human kindness over his critics. *Tricked into Marriage* is a case of the biter bit. These three novels are studies of minds warped by moral faults. The mind overbalanced by some delusion is studied

in *Licentiate Glass* and in the personal history of Don
Quixote, which must originally have resembled an
exemplary novel.

The curious Impertinent is a study of morbid
psychology, taking its rise from the *Orlando Furioso*;
and the history of *Cardenio and Dorotea*—an examination of the untoward effects of timidity—received
the honour of furnishing a sub-plot to *Don Quixote*.
Herein lies the historical significance of the novels
of the second epoch, which straddle the immortal
work before and after. They represent Cervantes
at the height of his powers as creator and observer
of life. His eye is unerring, and for the time his
art is not unduly influenced either by his romanticism or artistic prejudices derived from his environment. It is not that he subserves the facts. His
didactic sense gives organization even to vice and
crime, and his sympathy for the fallen sheds a warm
glow round his characters. The savage cynicism of
Quevedo or the drab realism of Mateo Alemán are
alien to his sunny genius. His eye sees and describes,
but his heart pardons and ennobles.

The novels of the third sort lie on a descending
parabola of genius. Their guarantee of truth is
still the Spanish life observed by their author, but
his mind had revolted against the tyranny of fact.
He sought a more plastic manner, in which more
of the success of the tale should be due to the
ingenious combinations effected by the author.
This is what some modern writers have dubbed
'creativeness', feeling a desire for free invention
like that which inspired the later exemplary novels.
It is the mood which led to the *Persiles*, and to

Cervantes' revolt against what he felt to be the narrow limits of the second part of *Don Quixote*, 'while he had skill, sufficiency and wit to treat of the whole universe' (ii. 44). The plots become more important in his eyes; but they tend to be conventional and to be concluded with too great a complaisance. His object is to provide honest recreation, and his portraits of well-to-do youths and discreet maidens have not the raciness of his Sevillan rascals. The language follows the same track, with a notable loss of dialogue.

The earliest piece in this style was *The Spanish Englishwoman*, of 1606. Use is even made of the fight at Les Trois Maries, but the conclusion is solidly located in Sevilla. The more important episodes occur in London—*terra incognita* to Cervantes—and he is not scrupulous about their realism so long as they serve his turn in the plot. In *The illustrious Kitchen-wench*, of 1608 (?), we find the two styles set side by side. Carriazo's career as a voluntary vagrant in Andalusia and his pranks in the squares of Toledo spring from observation, but the discreetly negative figure of Constanza and the progress of Avendaño's wooing are mere matchmaking. In the Second Part of *Don Quixote* the history of Ricote makes capital from the revived interest in Moorish things due to the edict of expulsion; its ending is happy, but botched. It is in *The little Gipsy* that we find this late romanticism full-blown, combining the urge to create a neat (though at bottom conventional) plot with some real knowledge of the ways and organization of gipsies. Yet the novel pleases. The author's affection glows and his style is golden, reminding us of *The Tempest*, and we can feel the same gratitude to him as to Shakespeare. He had given us his *Rinconete* and *Dogs' Colloquy*, and it was his right to offer other fare. If he now saw life less keenly, he saw it with greater love. The haze is restful, kindliness embraces all, and there is a sense of fruition. Such things are to be enjoyed with thankfulness as well as the vivacity, immediacy, bustle, and veracity of the great period.

THE BIRTH OF *DON QUIXOTE*

En un lugar de la Mancha, de cuyo nombre no quiero acordarme

IT was the skill and moral purpose of the exemplary novelist, vivified by a rich idea, which gave birth to *Don Quixote*.

All creative works sprout from a germinal idea. The process of inspiration seems mysterious to the layman, but, if we are to credit Edgar Allan Poe, it does not in itself constitute a merit in the artist. Ideas come to us all—in our baths, when drowsy, in the middle of action, struck from the flint of conversation. What distinguishes the common man from the artist is the latter's genius for perceiving the possibilities of the idea, and still more his skill in working them out. It is in this laborious process of roughing out, cancelling, revising, and finally approving the various implications of the original thought that the craft of letters consists, and in this way literary genius also is an infinite capacity for taking pains. The idea which lies behind *Don Quixote* did not lead to important work in the *Interlude of Ballads*, to which we shall recur later, but only when squeezed for sap by Cervantes. It was of a sort that recurred to him frequently, though in the other cases the possibilities seemed more limited. Cervantes tended it with the care of one resolved to teach his generation and with the verbal and plastic skill of his perfected style; and *Don Quixote*, far from being an accident in his literary life, proves to have been its almost necessary consequence. The fact has been obscured by the slavish observance of late date for the *Exemplary Novels*. Their appearance in

1613 was momentous for Cervantes' imitators and admirers, but they had, in many important cases, taken effect in his own art ten or twenty years earlier. He had reached the zenith of his skill as an exemplary novelist when he sat down to write *Don Quixote*, and what he had in mind to write was, in the first instance, an exemplary novel.

We have seen that Cervantes, like Shakespeare, was fascinated by varieties of morbid psychology. The mind warped by some injurious passion or unhinged by a strange delusion seemed to open up its depth to his discerning and sympathetic glance. The vicious principle produced odd effects which were signs of unsuspected possibilities of our nature, and it threw into striking relief the sounder qualities. The study of the morbid led to a truer appreciation of the sane, just as sunspots reveal forces which the photosphere conceals. By this path Cervantes rose to be a supreme delineator of human character, by shifting the balance of interest from plot to personality, partly against his own preferences. By taste Cervantes remained a great romancer, as the *Persiles* proves; but by a truer instinct he became the creator of the Novel.

In the simplest instances this idea of monomania is clothed in mere anecdotes. Cervantes speaks of a Sevillan lunatic who made it his business to puff dogs out like balloons, and another who dropped flagstones on them in Córdoba. The possibilities are greater when the folly has an intellectual aspect, as in the case of the man who, being sensible in every other respect, believed himself to be the god Neptune. In this case, also recorded in *Don Quixote* ii, the anecdote is longer and has more particulars. The unfortunate man had had a distinguished career, being a graduate of Osuna; he was a Canonist. The theme leads to a discussion which raises our esteem for his intelligence and discretion. Another, a raging lunatic, is introduced as a foil, and then comes the abrupt, bathetic plunge into foolishness. Still greater expectations might have been raised by the four contrasted madmen of the end of *The Dogs' Colloquy*: an alchemist, a poet, a mathematician, an arbitrist, as it was then called, or in eighteenth-century English, a 'projector'. The poet had composed an epos in thirty-two years of toil; twenty of composition, and twelve of fermentation. It was

'grand in the subject, admirable and new in the invention, grave in verse, amusing in its episodes, marvellously distributed, inasmuch as the beginning responded to the middle and end, and so constituted a lofty, sonorous, heroic, delightful, and substantial poem.'

All the history of King Arthur for which Turpin's authority could not be found was set forth by this poem in a variety of metres, with trisyllabic rhyme, and never a verb in rhyme. The mathematician had yearned for the mathematically impossible during twenty-two years; and the alchemist required only two months' more work to find the philosophers' stone. As for the 'arbitrist' or 'projector' or (as we might say) publicist, he had devised a scheme for paying off the Spanish national debt by means of monthly meatless days. He lived too soon, coming before our time when every folly is practical politics.

These thumbnail sketches were not developed, though Swift later made use of others like them.

Cervantes left them in their husk, and worked out more fully an intrinsically poorer idea in *Licentiate Glass*. The idea of a man who thinks himself made of glass does not appear to have come to Cervantes from the contemporary case of Carl Barth, since scholars declare the dates forbid this. He may have taken a hint from a phrase in Benvenuto Cellini's autobiography, or have followed some unknown model, or have freely invented the motif. It leads to one or two obvious developments: the lunatic is terrified of breaking, and he wears specially loose clothes, lies on straw, and travels in panniers. Cervantes does all that can be done with his datum, but his novelette passes from the folly to the sanity of its hero. He captures the reader's warmest esteem; for Tomás Rodaja was an intelligent boy, avid to learn and eager for honest advancement, a brilliant graduate of Salamanca but without losing the qualities of a soldier and gentleman, and after the best of educations in books and travel he was about to settle to the world's serious tasks, when the criminal infatuation of a woman destroyed his health and bewildered his reason. Though strangely foolish in part, he remained clear and incisive in his general outlook; his criticisms of society were pointed and entertaining (though somewhat conventional), and his mental isolation gave him some privileges as a critic. Finally a good man restores him the full use of his reason, and a bad world finds him no longer amusing, so that his whole profit from his sanity is to rush to death in Flanders. In all this *Licentiate Glass* is remarkably like *Don Quixote*, and may be called a preliminary sketch. It is so logically, though not in point of time, for the time of composition would seem to have been four or five years later than 1605. The novelette combines two things essential to the novel: the study of an unbalanced judgement and the criticism of society.

Chivalresque folly had been embodied, before Cervantes imagined Don Quixote, in the Bartolo of an anonymous *Interlude of Ballads*.[1] The work has been very variously related to *Don Quixote*, some attributing it to Cervantes and most disagreeing, while some hold it for a feeble imitation and others for a source. The line we take must therefore be cut boldly through some opinions, though we believe it conforms both to the better reason and to the best authorities. The first printed edition is dated 1611, but the internal allusions strongly suggest the age of the Armada (1588). Bartolo plans to attack Drake and Queen Elizabeth:

> my brother Bartolo
> to England is gone,
> to slaughter the Drake
> and capture the Queen.

The feat was impossible after 1596, and not practicable after 1588. The ballads quoted belong, all but three, to the period 1580–5. These others appeared in print in 1589, 1593, and 1597, but may have been known earlier. Mention made of the *romancero*, or totality of ballads, need not imply the existence of the *Romancero general* of 1600, since

---

[1] R. Menéndez Pidal, *Un Aspecto en la Elaboración del Quijote*, Madrid, 1920, and J. Millé y Giménez, *Sobre la Génesis del Quijote*, Barcelona, 1930. Text in *El Hospital de los Podridos*, ed. D. Alonso, Madrid, 1936.

the word had appeared in titles of books as early
as 1578. It is superfluous to endeavour to tip the
balance in favour of 1588 by supposing, as Sr. Millé
has done, that the initiate might have seen in this
farce a likeness to the doings of a wild young poet
named Lope de Vega in that year; nor should we
stress too much the possibility that the interlude
arose in 1597 and so perhaps immediately before
Don Quixote. For the prison in which the novel was
conceived was most likely the Royal Prison of Sevilla,
where Cervantes lay in 1597, an institution mor-
dantly described in an interlude of that name which
some have attributed to the master.

What had Cervantes to learn from the *Interlude
of Ballads*? Not much, we ought frankly to confess.
It is crude, though spirited. Ballads of chivalry
have deprived Bartolo of his wits. With Bandurrio
for squire he leaves his young wife for the wars,
saddling an ass and enclosed in ridiculous armour.
In the open fields he interferes in a lovers' tiff, but
the young gallant seizes his lance and lays him flat.
His friends find him and carry him home, the while
he recites passages from the ballads of *Valdovinos*
and *Abindarráez* appropriate to his case, ending in a
pell-mell of disparate lines. But *Don Quixote* begins
firmly as an attack on romances of chivalry. In the
second and fifth chapters the ballads get the upper
hand, as the hero recites *Lancelot* and *Constancy* on
approaching the inn, and *Valdovinos* and *Abindarráez*
in his overthrow. His interference with Juan Haldudo, engaged in whipping Andresillo, and his overthrow by the Murcian merchants, are incidents not
wholly unlike those offered by the farce. But there

is no inescapable influence of the interlude on the novel. It *might* have suggested the notion of an attack on works of chivalry; it *might* have turned aside a work already begun, so that the immediate target should be ballads, not novels; or this *might* have been due simply to the wit of Cervantes questing among the ludicrous resources of his theme.

At the outset Cervantes' vision extended as far as the episode of the windmills in the seventh chapter, but, despite the precedent of the *Interlude*, he had not thought of a squire. Without Sancho Panza none of the dominant notes of the novel are quite firmly struck; there is not the same critique of reality, nor the same savoury conversations. The Scrutiny of the Books has not taken place, and though the satire is clearly directed against romances of chivalry, *Amadís de Gaula* and *Orlando Furioso* have not yet their pre-eminence. On the contrary, the main attack promises to be against Feliciano de Silva, who had added pastoral conventions to chivalry, and was the master of a strangely contorted style. Instead of the assured lines of the rest of the novel, the first five chapters consist of a number of joyous experiments, some of which were not further developed. In them the author's mind quests after his veritable subject. For the moment he proposes to execute a *novella* of an exemplary kind, showing briefly the harm that comes from an unregulated passion for fiction. With the Scrutiny of the Books and the entry of Sancho the work lengthens into the great novel we know; but size alone would not mark it off from the *Exemplary Novels*. Cervantes proposed to add a sequel to

Rinconete and Cortadillo, and *The Dogs' Colloquy* (already extending to a hundred pages of normal print) is half its logical length. But length led to complexity, as the problem of maintaining interest in the narrative became ever more insistent, and so the novel abandoned the simplicity which marks the short-story plot.

The author's eye first falls on his hero, preparing for battle in his antique armament. Azorín has compared him with the portrait of Don Rodrigo Pacheco in the church of Argamasilla de Alba, considered by the natives to be Don Quixote's proto-type. Spanish gentlemen painted by El Greco are not unlike, and the author must have borrowed from his own appearance. He would have been fifty years of age in 1597, and his nose was aqui-line and moustaches long. He too read to excess, and his wits had become sterile and ill-balanced through age, oblivion, and imprisonment. He in-sists on the resemblance:

'What could my sterile, ill-equipped wit beget but the history of a nut-dry whimsical child, beset by a diversity of thoughts never imagined by any other, fit product of a prison where all discomfort dwells and all kinds of noise abide? Calm, a cheerful spot, the beauty of the country, the serenity of the skies, the murmuring of brooks, quietude of spirit— these greatly help the most sterile muses to prove fecund and offer to the world progeny that fills it with wonder and delight.

'Now, at the end of so many years of slumber in the silence of oblivion, I come forward with all my years on my back, with a legend as dry as esparto grass, poor in inven-tion, defective in style, lacking wit, erudition and doctrine, without quotations in the margin or annotations at the back.'

The same physical particulars are found in Don
Quixote's sane counterpart, Don Diego de Miranda;
fifty years of age, with few white hairs, aquiline
features, and a gravely cheerful glance.

It is books of chivalry, not ballads, that first
swim into our ken, and the first model is the egre-
gious Feliciano de Silva. The hero is enraptured
by 'The reason for the unreason done to my reason,
so weakens my reason that with reason I make
complaint of your beauty' and 'the high heavens
with the stars which divinely strengthen you with
divinity, and make you deserving of the desert your
greatness deserves'. Thus in its first moments the
novel promises to become a parody of a meretricious
style, and the parody continues for a chapter or two
more. It is the grandiloquence of the romances
that springs to mind as Don Quixote sallies from
his back gate:

'Scarcely had ruddy Apollo extended over the face of
the wide and spacious earth the gilded fibres of his lovely
hair, and no sooner had the small variegated birds with
their harping tongues saluted with sweet mellifluous harmony
the coming of rosy Aurora, who, abandoning the soft couch
of her jealous husband, revealed herself through the doors
and balconies of the Manchegan horizon to mortal men,
when the famous knight Don Quixote de la Mancha,
leaving the feather-bed of idleness, mounted his famous
horse Rocinante, and began to travel over the famous old
plain of Montiel' (i. 2).

This amounts to no more than 'Don Quixote
mounted at dawn', but the point of the joke lies in
the redundant eloquence customary among knights
errant. This aureate style of the late fifteenth and

early sixteenth centuries had become unintelligible
to the average Spaniard, especially as it was accompanied by archaisms of pronunciation, vocabulary,
and syntax. The two wantons at the inn of Puerto
Lápiche are as much bewildered by the *ff, ca, non,
sandez,* and *las vuestras* of the language as by Don
Quixote's overwhelming, but misplaced, courtliness.
The novel at this time was setting in the direction of
verbal parody, for its hero had not yet settled into
his style. In later chapters he still uses a courtly,
altisonant diction, but not one cut off from his surroundings. There are times, too, when the essential
peasant peeps out, as in his remark to the innkeeper
that 'the weight of arms cannot be borne without
looking after the guts'.

Don Quixote is, at this period, thrilling with the
first intoxication of liberty, and he explores, like his
creator, all the rich and varied possibilities of his
folly. So the third chapter is quite unlike the second.
It gives the first of a long line of savoury conversations which grow in significance for the novel, and
the innkeeper, though a worse thief than Cacus, pre-
figures Sancho. In the fullness of time the novel
lived by dialogue, since through conversations the
author explored the nature of truth. In this early
chapter the essence of the method is revealed. The
facts are known to the reader, together with the
misconstruction made by Don Quixote; but the
innkeeper adds another misconstruction due to certain causes which are revealed to the reader. We
have, therefore, no such crude opposition of fact
and delusion as in the *Interlude of Ballads*, but two
human constructions both different from fact. This

innkeeper is a rogue from Sevilla and he outlines the map of Spanish roguery, as we find it in *The happy Ruffian*, *Rinconete*, and *The Dogs' Colloquy*. The Andalusian attachment is a link with Cervantes' earlier work, since, taken as a whole, *Don Quixote* is rather pan-Hispanic than Andalusian.

It is with the fourth chapter that the adventure begins. It is at this point that the resemblance to the *Interlude of Ballads* is most noticeable, the more so that *Valdovinos* and *Abindarráez* are common to both. Yet the resemblance may be fortuitous, and certainly Cervantes surpassed his predecessor. With an apparent triumph over Juan Haldudo and excusable defeat by the Murcian merchants, the Knight is not to be shaken out of his folly. The use of ballads at this point was convenient, since they were present to the minds of all readers and were calculated to make a maximum appeal. It is also in keeping with the exploratory manner of these first chapters. Later in the First Part they sink to, so to say, the subconscious, but in the Second they provide the frame for the important episodes of Montesinos' Cave and Clavileño.

The geography of this section is difficult, as we have remarked elsewhere. It would appear that the author has omitted one night, since the Housekeeper and Niece speak of an absence of three days. Don Quixote sallied out to the South and reached a point in the North-West; he returned from the North-East. To make a difficulty of this is to demand a consistency that interested Cervantes very little; 'for suppose they do detect the lie they won't cut off the hand you wrote it with.' He throws in detail because his mind crystallizes ideas into pictures. He wants an inn; let it be Puerto Lápiche, on the road to Sevilla. Sevillan muleteers and a Sevillan rogue come to hand. Later he wants merchants; let them be travelling in silks to Murcia, though the road runs in a different direction. Sancho Panza, his wife, and even Don Quixote himself are revealed in the same way, as their creator's glance becomes focused on this or that particular. The important fact is the intensity and plasticity of the Cervantine genius. In the prologue he has to say that he is about to write but does not know what. Immediately a complete picture springs to his mind: 'hesitating, paper in front, pen behind my ear, elbow on the desk, hand on jaw, thinking what to say.'

THE GROWTH OF *DON QUIXOTE*

No sólo la dulzura de su verdadera historia, sino de los cuentos y episodios della, que, en parte, no son menos agradables y artificiosos y verdaderos que la misma historia.

THE idea which inspired *Don Quixote* differed from others not in kind nor in development, but in a greater intrinsic richness. During the canter taken round the field in the first five chapters it had become apparent that the chivalresque folly involved a parody of the archaic and rhetorical style of successful romances, but through the ballads a direct appeal could be made to the whole public. Through the flame of a single obsession could be seen a bizarre spectrum of the human mind. The afflicted hero had a certain necessary nobility, and even some resemblance to his creator, and his adventures had already brought together a rich assortment of Spanish types. As his madness affected the nature of truth, it had vast possibilities as a criticism of life. It was time to take stock, and to set a course through the episodes and digressions that had begun to crowd Cervantes' imagination.

Stock-taking is the business of the Scrutiny of the Books (i. 6). It is really a second treatment of this subject, since the first chapter had already indicated the principal works concerned. In that case the first mention had been of Feliciano de Silva, author of four romances in the *Amadís* cycle. He was famous for sophisticated prose, and for having mingled the chivalresque and pastoral traditions by the introduction of Darinel. Then follow the romances of the Spanish series: *Belianís, Palmerín of England, Amadís.* After a mention of Bernardo del Carpio as Roland's conqueror, Cervantes had then passed to Pulci's *Morgante* and the *Orlandos* of Ariosto and Boiardo, represented in Spain by *The Mirror of Chivalry.* Traditional ballads embodied most of this material in a form vulgarly accessible.

The effect of the Scrutiny was not to modify this brief list of works actually influencing the construction of the work. The matter is essentially simpler. Cervantes' debt to the *Amadís* and the *Orlando Furioso*[1] outweighs all other considerations. The other novels of each cycle are subsidiary to these two, and, on the whole, it is the Italian source which is the more fruitful. *Don Quixote* is an *Orlando Furioso* and *Innamorato* in prose. Its chapters are cantos, which often begin with moral reflections in Ariosto's manner and end on effective points of suspension. The Biscayan and our hero are suspended with swords in air like the Argalia and Ferragut of Boiardo. The affair of Mambrino's helmet is due to conflation of Boiardo with Ariosto; it begins as a chance allusion in the tenth chapter, gives the novel one of its principal episodes in the twenty-first, and returns as cause of the mêlée at the inn (i. 44–5). The troops of merino sheep are reviewed by Don Quixote in the eighteenth chapter in the serio-comic style of Boiardo's siege of Albracà (*Orl. Inn.* 1. x). In the twenty-fifth chapter the question arises as to whether Amadís or Orlando be the better model for the frenzy of the Sierra Morena.

[1] On Cervantes' relations with Italy see Al. Popescu-Telega, *Cervantes și Italia*, Craiova, Rămuri, 1931.

Don Quixote prefers Amadís, who was more melancholy than mad; but to get rid of Sancho he gave some cartwheels in the style of the furious Orlando, and then settled into a quiescence that does not belong entirely to either hero. It was Ariosto who, by his interlude of Angelica and Medoro, had authorized the mingling of heroic and pastoral with more effect than Feliciano de Silva. The hubbub at the inn corresponded to the discord of Agramante's host (i. 45); Sancho lost his ass, according to his own account, by a trick of Brunello's (ii. 4; cf. *Orl. Fur.* xxvii); Merlin and the cave, together with the flying horse, have their antecedents in Ariosto as well as in Spanish tradition. This sort of correspondence is, however, vastly less significant than Cervantes' indebtedness for technique and temper. Based on the maxim that ' nature is lovely in variety ', Cervantes seeks and attains the astonishing virtuosity of Ariosto, varying his motifs and intricately weaving his strands. Boiardo had clothed his parody of chivalry with elegance and a certain nobility; qualities retained by Ariosto with the more poignant sentiment of regret for what was not only unattainable, but had never existed.

> Great-hearted goodness of those ancient knights,

he had sung, but he had not realized it so humanely as Don Quixote. Coincidence of detail is but the sign of a more fundamental agreement between the ironical genius who opened the age of Renaissance epic poetry and him who brought it to a brave, but disillusioned, close.

Though not changed, the course of the novel

was confirmed by the Scrutiny of the Books, and it no longer reveals (we are speaking of the main action) the almost boyish experimentalism of the first five chapters. The satire is one of character and society, not of words. New responsibilities weighed on the author as he saw his short story lengthening into an *historia*, with its demand for a more complex appeal to sustain the flagging interest of its readers. Its basis was also generalized and widened. The books in Don Quixote's library were not only chivalresque. He had also pastoral novels in a complete set from the *Diana* of Montemayor to the *Shepherd of Iberia* of 1591. This is the latest date given by his collection, and it is significant that the mention of Luis Barahona de Soto's *Angelica's Tears* (1586) should not have led to a note on Lope de Vega's *Angelica's Beauty* (1602). These works belong to the class of Italianate epics, and there were *Bernardo del Carpio* and *Roncesvalles* in the Spanish vein. Don Quixote's interest in the epos embraced also Ercilla's *Araucana*, Rufo's *Austriada*, and Cristóbal de Virués' *Monserrate*. He also possessed Padilla's *Treasure* of 1580 and Maldonado's *Song-book* of 1586, lyrical collections which justified his dissertation on poetry in the second part of the novel. But in all this library there was only one book of solid history,[1] and the disproportionate appeal to the imagination is palpable. Don Diego de Miranda, our Knight's sane counterpart, had a

---

[1] D. Luis de Ávila is mentioned in chapter 7. He wrote on the German wars of Charles V (1546). But it is easy to believe in a slip of the author's pen, and that the person intended was Don Luis de Zapata, author of an epic on the Emperor.

library which we may suppose chosen on a sound criterion.

'I have up to six dozen books, some in Spanish, some in Latin, some of history, others of devotion. Novels of chivalry have not entered the threshold of my door. I take up the profane more than the devout, provided that they give honest entertainment and please by their language and cause wonder and suspense by their invention. There are few such in Spain.'

In short, it is not so much the presence of chivalrous novels that proved disastrous to Don Quixote, as his surrender to all forms of fiction, without any solid corrective. He was as ready to turn shepherd as knight, and would gladly argue for poetry as a substitute for life.

The chivalrous novels and poems mentioned range from the *Amadís* of 1508 to *Angelica's Tears* of 1586, and the pastorals from 1559 to 1591. Ercilla's *Araucana* was completed in 1590. These are the last dates to be inferred for Don Quixote's reading, and (to some extent) for that which so profoundly affected Cervantes. The picaresque novel of *Guzmán de Alfarache* (1599) is not mentioned, though it might not have proved welcome here. It is true that *Lazarillo de Tormes* (1554) has to wait until the Second Part for a citation, and there was too much realism in the picaresque tradition to have appealed to the Manchegan. The bracket for the composition of the First Part has to be extended to 1591–1602, but the appearance in the latter year of Lope de Vega's *Angelica's Beauty* and Cristóbal de Figueroa's *Pastor Fido* could hardly have been passed over. Unmentioned also is Lope de Vega's *Arcadia* of 1598. The indications help to fix the year 1597, when Cervantes suffered a period of imprisonment in the Royal Prison of Sevilla, as the date of the plan and partial execution of this work.

In its further development *Don Quixote* should be studied under three principal aspects : its external form, the resources of the narrator, and the inner development of his persons.

The First Part of *Don Quixote* is characterized by the number of strands that have gone to its making.[1] In the Second Part an attempt has been made to weave the pattern from one design, but the alien matter is still visible, though more subtly blended. Cervantes viewed his first volume apprehensively. This 'nut-dry' story about a whimsical Manchegan might not please ; let critics be pacified by examples of pastoral and exemplary skill and glimpses of every sort of entertainment. The reader will then not doubt but that the author has ' skill, sufficiency, and wit to treat of the whole universe', and he will bless him not only for the veracious history, but for the tales and episodes within it. Sharp criticism of *The curious Impertinent* taught Cervantes better. For the Second Part he proposed the formula 'Let Don Quixote attack and Sancho talk'. But his difficulty remained on foot, viz. how to keep sweet a long narrative about a limited number of persons and topics. It was against Nature that this should be done without tedium, in view of the maxim that

[1] See the articles on this subject by J. D. M. Ford in the *Mélanges Jeanroy* and by Milton Buchanan in the *Bonilla Homenaje*.

Nature herself needed variety: *per troppo variar Natura è bella.* Despite his new intention, therefore, Cervantes returns to the episodic treatment in the Second Part also, though with a new subtlety and skill. Having finished his great novel, he allowed such space to episodes in his *Persiles and Sigismunda* as to shatter that romance into fragments.

In respect of handling of plot the antecedents of *Don Quixote* are to be found not in the *Exemplary Novels* but in the plays. Multiple plots appealed to him, since they were evidence of his own creative ingenuity; and he supposed that they equally delighted his hearers. The *Numantia* is concerned with the national struggle and with a love affair. *The Traffic of Algiers* employs the motif of 'crossed lovers' only as a central knot to tie a number of different interests. In *The Bagnios* two plots of equal importance are developed; in *The Grand Sultana* there are two sub-plots, one romantic and one farcical, to divert us alongside the main action. The complexity of plot rises to a fantastic extreme in *Love's Labyrinth*. In the *Galatea* the ostensible fable of Elicio and Galatea is no more than an envelope enclosing many different actions, all on the same plane of interest. The plot of a short story is necessarily simple, but the broadening of the narrative stream in *Don Quixote* led to divided currents and episodic islands.

A second exemplary theme gave the sub-plot. It is the matter of *Cardenio or Timidity*, which fills chapters 22–4, 27–8, 36. This is entitled to rank beside the main adventure not so much because the sight of Cardenio's folly puts Don Quixote in mind of

the melancholy of Beltenebros, as because Dorotea
is required to pass from a minor role in the affair
of Cardenio to a major part in the restoration of the
Knight to his home. She, at least, enters into the
main stream of adventure, though the others remain
spectators. Two exemplary novels are intercalated
in the romance. *The Story of the captive Captain*
(i. 39–42) is a rehandling of the second plot of *The
Bagnios* and is exemplary in the earlier style. As the
Captain joins the company of travellers, his affairs
are not wholly irrelevant to the action, and an appendix (*The Muleteer*, i. 43–6) is tacked on by the
flimsiest of pretexts. The other exemplary novelette
is the famous *Curious Impertinent* (i. 32–5), which is
found in a valise by mine host of the inn. The story is
one of the best, but Cervantes himself admitted it had
nothing to do with the case. A pastoral novelette,
Grisóstomo and Marcela (i. 12–14), has a poem to
Olalla for preface (i. 11), and there is the anecdote
of *The fair Leandra* (i. 51) which threatens to dis-
locate the narrative at its close. The Scrutiny of
the Books (i. 6), the discourse of Arms and Letters
(i. 37–8), and the Canon's disquisition on the
Novel and Drama (i. 47–8), are legitimate digressions which serve to illuminate the protagonist's
character.

The effect of these interruptions is that the hero's
control of his own adventures is loosened after the
twenty-seventh chapter, and the development of his
action is strained through a bog of foreign matter.
Nor are the interpolations congruent with the main
history. Some belong to an idealistic convention
that jars in a realistic setting; in others it is the

motivation which rings false, or some of the devices
used to hurry on the plot; and yet in others, having nothing else to blame, we complain of sheer
irrelevance. Cervantes himself was aware of these
difficulties, and not only when he came to write the
Second Part. When he did so, he had the great
advantage of knowing good from evil. Let us remember that none even of the *Exemplary Novels* had been
placed before the great public in 1605, and that
Don Quixote was something entirely new in literature.
The author, obfuscated by his natural affection for
all his children, could not form so clear an idea of
the merits of the novel until he had experienced the
rush of public affection for his Manchegan. His
aesthetic preceptors urged him to produce 'a web
woven of various fair strands' (i. 47). Composition
was still medieval, and medieval text-books had so
stressed the need for variety that almost all longer
works lacked unity. The supreme consecration had
been given by the *Orlando Furioso*, turning into new
streams of narrative, large or small, with every canto,
and yet with such exquisite skill and proportion that
the reader is as little distracted as bored. In the
Araucana Alonso de Ercilla had attempted to substitute truth for fable, but he had wearied of the
dull recital of slaughter. First borrowing some
women from Ariosto in order to invest his Arau-
canian braves with some social interest, he had
wandered into idylls and scenes of witchcraft, not
to mention the recital of European battles. His
failure, despite great talent, to plough a straight
and narrow furrow of truth must have served to con-
firm, in the mind of his sincere admirer Cervantes,

the pre-eminence of the Ariostean art of narrative. So he praises his plot and his digressions:

'So happy and fortunate were the times which cast into the world the most audacious of knights, Don Quixote de la Mancha, for not only do we enjoy in this our age, which grievously needs pleasant entertainment, the sweetness of his veritable history, but also its tales and episodes, not less agreeable, in part, or artful or true than the story itself.' (i. 28.)

The novelist's art was to keep the ball rolling: to observe proportion, swing out and into the narrative with virtuosity, and carry all forward on an agreeable current of language. Relevance was left unexamined; but it had become a principle with the Second Part. It is there stated that *The curious Impertinent* was 'not bad nor badly told, but not appropriate nor relevant to the history of Don Quixote' (ii. 3). The Knight added: 'I don't know what induced the author to make use of alien stories and tales, when there were so many of mine to be written.' 'Let us have more quixotries: let Don Quixote attack and Sancho talk.' Though this is the formula of the Second Part, it does not cover its practice. *Camacho's Wedding* (ii. 19–21) is a pastoral in a more realistic style, into which Don Quixote and Sancho happen to stumble; and *The History of the Moor Ricote* (ii. 54, 63, 65) is irrelevant to their affairs, though ingeniously attached by external ties to Sancho Panza. Similarly, the gory little episode of *Claudia Jerónima* (ii. 60) is essentially irrelevant. As for the rest of the plot, there is an evident desire to organize its incidents. It is strung out along a road, like so many of those used

by this author; and 'long travels always involve a
diversity of events'. In the First Part these events
merely succeed one another, being subject only to
acceptance or rejection; but in the Second they
rise to two climaxes, namely the two battles with
Sansón Carrasco, and during twenty-seven chapters
are controlled by a single ducal household. The
first emotion which Don Quixote feels on leaving
that house is of a recovered liberty, and is there a
reader who does not sympathize with him? The
ducal atmosphere had proved heavy, with its smart
duchess, officious majordomo, stupid duenna, and
idle lackeys and wenches; and we are glad to issue
again into the strong Spanish sunlight and to meet
the genuine Spanish people.

So Cervantes' last word is not that with which he
began the Second Part. He writes (ii. 44):

'They say that when, in the proper original of this history,
Cid Hamete reached this chapter, his interpreter did not
translate him literatim. The Moor made a sort of complaint
against himself for having taken in hand so limited and dry
a matter as this of Don Quixote, for he thought he must
always talk about him and Sancho, without risking an
expansion into graver or more amusing episodes and digressions. He said that it was an intolerable toil to keep his
mind, hand and pen always writing about one subject and
speaking through the mouths of a limited number of characters. This was unprofitable to the author, who, in the first
part of the novel, had made use of certain short stories (such
as *The curious Impertinent* and *The captive Captain*) in order
to avoid this inconvenience. They are, so to speak, separate
from the story, since the others occurred to Don Quixote
himself, and could not but be written down. So he was not
willing to insert loose or adhesive stories in this second part,

but only some episodes like them, begotten of the events of the narrative itself, and even these to a limited extent and with only the words needed to declare them. So he contains and encloses himself within the narrow limits of his narrative, though with skill, sufficiency and wit to treat of the whole world, and he begs that his work be not despised, but that he be praised not for what he writes, but for what he refrains from writing.'

The novelist's dilemma thus remained on foot. He must either distract or bore his readers, and be condemned for the one or the other. The ducal tract in the Second Part does tend to become monotonous, or at least constrictive. The irrelevances in the First add to the pageant of the Spanish roads, though not always in realistic outline, for they give us genuine goatherds and sham shepherds, lords and ladies a little out of drawing, a romanticized captive and some genuine galley-slaves, an oversensitive Italian, a flirt, a boy much in love, &c. Quite apart from precepts as to unity of plot, fullness of life has a claim on the novelist; and in the First Part his horn overflows with joyous excess.

The skill and resource shown by Cervantes in keeping the story moving have been admirably studied by M. Paul Hazard[1] and need not be laboured here. A full commentary would extend over the whole vast length of the two volumes. There is an inevitable sameness in the hero's adventures, which are all based on the shock of disillusionment, but there is no sameness in the details. Don Quixote rushes to attack the whirling windmills, but in the episode of the fulling hammers he is

[1] P. Hazard, *Don Quichotte de Cervantes*, Paris, Mellottée, n.d.

quiescent. He wins apparent victories and his de-
feats are ingeniously excused. When he triumphs,
Sancho is beaten. The episode of Mambrino's
helmet is conceived in a vein of exalted romanticism,
except by the luckless barber, and is immediately
followed by the realistic affair of the galley-slaves.
In this respect the first part is superior to the second,
since once matters come into the hands of the
Duchess and Butler, the narrative of hoaxes betrays
a greater sameness. Cervantes remarks that 'there
is not much credit in deceiving a trustful soul' (ii.
41), and when Altisidora's capers become at last a
stupid persecution, he opines that 'the Duke and
Duchess were not far from looking silly' (ii. 70).
It is one of the signs of loss of power, after the anger
which Avellaneda's continuation inspired in the
author, that Cervantes should drive a herd of swine
over Don Quixote and Sancho in chapter 68, though
he had sent over a herd of bulls in the 58th. But
when he is writing at his best there is no such
monotony. Consider the differences in detail between
the duels with the Biscayan and the Barber, between
the Knight of the Mirrors and the Knight of the
White Moon, though both these are the same Sansón
Carrasco. Consider also that ballads of identical
texture yield episodes so distinct as the Puppet Play
and Montesinos' Cave. A ballad had said:

> Never was a knight-at-arms
> by fair ladies entertained
> half so well as Lancelot
> when from Brittany he came;
> welcomed him fair demoiselles
> and his nag fair courtly dames.

The ballad gives totally different results when, on the one hand, Don Quixote entrusts Rocinante to the two wantons of Puerto Lápiche in a courtly speech, and, on the other, Sancho Panza endeavours to hand Dapple over to the duenna Rodríguez.

This ability to keep the story moving, we think, should be connected with the obscure Cervantine doctrine of verisimilitude. His point of departure is the Aristotelean distinction between poetry and history; poetry deals not with the true but with that which has verisimilitude, and in so doing it creates something truer, because more universal, than history. His immediate source was, no doubt, the poetics of El Pinciano. Verisimilitude extends so far as to include not only the possible but even the impossible. The author must make a prudent selection, because some things are too great to be suitable subjects and others are too base: ' everything written in a history is recommended by the savour of truth it contains, but this is not the case with fiction; the incidents of fiction must be tricked out so accurately and tastefully and with such verisimilitude as to form a genuine harmony, in spite of falsehood, which makes a dissonance in the understanding.' [1] The words are not entirely clear. The proposition seems to be that all truth is consonant with the understanding, and all falsehood dissonant; but things not actually true can be combined in the likeness of truth and so achieve a genuine harmony. Inasmuch as their measure of truth is universal, they may transcend the particular truthfulness of history.

[1] *Persiles*, iii. 16.

Hence Cervantes is able to combine a passion for the pastoral novel with a clear knowledge of its unreality. The nymphs and shepherds who gathered by the banks of the Tagus belong to the category of impossibles, and in the preface to the *Galatea* Cervantes frankly admits that he does not look for credence; but they are like the truth about the elegant intercourse of ladies and gentlemen, and they have more freedom, under their convention, to develop such universals as Leone Ebreo's theory of love. Or again: in *The Grand Sultana* there is a farcical scene in which a young man is discovered among the Grand Turk's wives. He says that he was formerly a woman, but prayed to Mohammed to be changed into a man because he thought men so much more fortunate. The Turk asks the Cadi if this is possible, and the Cadi says, ' Yes, indeed, and without a miracle.' Now under what conditions is this either true or like the truth? Clearly only under conditions of the wildest farce. Cervantes would not have ventured to tell such a story of Spain, but in Constantinople, Norway, or Scotland there is more scope for the imagination. In the *Cardenio* story we have a scene in which Fernando, son of a grandee, is betrothed by night in great secrecy to Luscinda, a gentleman's daughter, her father being present and assenting. Clearly no father would assent under such circumstances, and the whole scene bears no resemblance to reality. What then is its verisimilitude? It is like the truth under the figure of romantic fiction, which has secret weddings for a stock episode, partly for the sake of the consequent mystery, and partly to avoid describing the more

prosaic procedure. These weddings consist only of
the exchange of vows, but sometimes there are
attendants, and in the case in point it suited Cervantes' convenience that the hidden Cardenio should
be tortured by a comparatively lengthy scene. He
was exploiting the romantic convention.

But if so, Cervantes has no real quarrel with
novels of chivalry, which were also like the truth
under their own convention. What pleasure is there
in hearing that 'a boy of sixteen slashes at a giant
as big as a tower and cuts him in two parts like
sugar paste'? Much for the Innkeeper and none
for the Canon. It is not the lie itself which proves
discordant, but the artlessness with which it is told,
for, as the Canon says, 'I have never seen a book
of chivalry making a single plot complete in all its
members, so that the middle corresponds with the
beginning, and the end with the beginning and
middle; they are rather formed of so many members that it would seem the authors propose to
form a chimera or monster rather than a well pro-
portioned figure.'

'In addition to this they are harsh in style, incredible in
their feats, lascivious in love scenes, gauche in courtesy,
tedious in battles, foolish in speeches, absurd in voyages,
and finally alien from all discreet artifice, and so deserve to
be ejected from the republic as vagabonds.'

Clearly it is the style which recommends the
matter, and pragmatic tests alone determine how
far verisimilitude extends. 'Fictitious fables must
be married to the reader's understanding', but if
that can be done, there is no reproach in fiction.
So long as the style will bear the narrative it can

proceed. This is not always the case with Cervantes, despite all his art, and the cause may be his excessive respect for precept and tradition. He seems to admit fictions under different conventions as if the licence to lie were without condition. Farce knows many stories as absurd as that of the young man and the Grand Turk, and it might well stand alone; but it clashes with a major plot which is concerned with the resistance of a Christian conscience in a Moslem land. We might accept some improbabilities in the history of Catalina de Oviedo if they served to advance this main theme; but we resent the intrusion of a quite alien romanticism. It is the same with the First Part of *Don Quixote*, where the patchiness is due not to more or less verisimilitude, but to differences of texture; differences which Cervantes was very careful to avoid in the Second Part.

The author was afraid lest the interest attaching to his main action should obscure the skill of the subordinate novelettes (ii. 44). Though they have been noticed in a previous chapter, it is right we should meet his convenience here. They are enough to have given half another volume of *Exemplary Novels*, and they have the same range and qualities. The history of Cardenio is a study of moral failure both here and in *The Comedy of Entertainment*. He is timid and his opponent is rash and overbearing; Luscinda is yielding but faithful, and Dorotea is ambitious. It would seem to have been difficult to find a frame for this situation, seeing that a quite new one is used for the play, for such extreme timidity in an otherwise gallant gentleman seems incomprehensible. The plots are somewhat forced, and the solutions unoriginal. In *The curious Impertinent* we encounter one of his best psychological studies, based on the *Orlando Furioso* (cantos 42 and 43), as the author acknowledges. There are two Moorish tales, the one from his early period, and the other from about 1610, when the Moors had again become topical. Intrinsically the story of Ricote is of no great verisimilitude, and its end is severely pruned. One cares little for the girl-pirate, though doubtless such were not wholly unknown; and the escape of Gregorio or Gaspar (whatever his name may have been) from a Moroccan harem in woman's dress requires more elaboration. Cervantes remarked on the necessity for brevity in these episodes, and the tale is particularly notable for the skill with which it is made to follow the trajectory of the main narrative. As for the pastorals, there is a world of difference between the history of Grisóstomo and that of Basilio; the latter is set firmly into the Spanish landscape, though the denouement is that of an Italian novelette.

These pieces occasionally add to length without increase of entertainment; some show signs of wilfulness in their invention, and their texture is unequal. But they do vary the main action and allow the Knight and the Squire to rest from their wanderings and form part of the general Spanish background to which they, in fact, belong. The intrusive material allows them a breathing-space, and at the same time lets the busy world into their adventures. The novel thus contains captives and sham shepherds, lovers and intriguers, viceroys and captains of galleys, all active on their own affairs. All Spain floods its pages and mingles with the curas, barbers, yangueses, Biscayans, innkeepers, servants, ecclesiastics, goatherds, galley-slaves, robbers, muleteers, and mutes of the highroads of La Mancha. Without interpolations our hero's follies would have been personal and local, like those of Licentiate Glass; with them Don Quixote is the symbol and centre of a busy, purposeful, deluded universe of men.

MASTER AND MAN

He comido su pan; quiérole bien.

NOTHING, of course, so enriched the novel as Don Quixote's resolve to turn back for Sancho Panza. It became transfigured. The worth of *Don Quixote* does not lie in the plot, however ingenious, nor in the narrative, however skilfully sustained, but in the revelation of the inner man. It is to Cervantes no less than to Shakespeare that the world owes proof that plot is but the outward semblance of character; and this is the essential step from the romance to the novel. Romance usually deals with fantastic activity, and the picaresque story treats of reality only under severe restrictions. Neither gives a view of human occupations in the round, because neither can, under its own conventions, offer a rounded personage. Such a person first appears in the figure of Don Quixote. He is no doubt at first a Jonsonian 'humour', or, as Spanish dramatists would have it, a *figurón*. In the first chapter he appears, amid vivid external details, possessed by one dominant passion. He is about fifty years of age, with curved nose and sweeping moustaches, dry and hollow, given to early rising and hunting. We know how he dressed and what he ate; and to this we must add his 'humour'.

'You must know that the aforesaid gentleman, when at ease (which was for most of the year) indulged in reading books of chivalry, with such zeal and pleasure that he almost wholly forgot the exercise of hunting, and even the administration of his property. His keenness and folly in this matter went so far that he sold many plots of corn land to buy books of chivalry, and so brought home all he could get.'

Vivid as this may be, our initial information about Don Quixote is less than we get concerning Licentiate Glass, whom we follow through half a life as boy, scholar, soldier, traveller, before he is plunged into his madness. His madness, however, was physical and unrevealing; but Alonso Quijada el Bueno was sick in spirit, and each new adventure served to reveal, not only his old obsession, but unsuspected qualities of the mind. Hence the discovery made in this novel: the mind declaring its many-sidedness in action.

This revelation is gradual, and to a large extent unforeseen by the author. There is no planned character in this work, but a continuous development like that of *Pilgrim's Progress* and *The Pickwick Papers*. A Madame Bovary is an increasingly precise view of the same thing; Don Quixote develops out of himself. The joyous, whole-hearted folly of the windmills has become the calculated folly of the Sierra Morena before half the First Part is out. In the Second Part his folly is hesitant and put upon him by others. The Knight himself sees truly, but is perplexed by his lingering prejudices. He is loath to fight the Knight of the Mirrors, and his rush on the puppets comes only at the crisis of an exciting play. He can recognize a peasant girl for a peasant and an inn for an inn, being no longer under the delusion of the First Part that they are damsels and castles. As a 'sane fool' he is already half-cured before he is overthrown on the shore at Barcelona; and it is a shamed and broken man who returns to

his village to die. A more gradual treatment might
have saved his life for the better furtherance of
justice, never so badly needed as in the Spain of the
Philips. However, the point is that we have not
always one and the same Don Quixote, even in
respect of his one obsession, but a hero who evolves
and becomes more complicatedly interesting. More
and more of reality comes into his ken, and the pole
of reality is occupied by Sancho Panza. But Sancho
also is not static. His master's notions first served
to confer on himself a sense of importance, since he
could become a mystagogos for lesser souls. But
custom, credulity, and chiefly affection caused him
to accept these ideals as everyday facts and part of
his own pragmatic creed. 'Anything may be', his
master had said, and Sancho reiterated 'Anything
may be', when the duchess confounded his judgement of even the most palpable truth. In time
master and man change places; and in the last agony
it is Sancho who believes in the possibility of rang-
ing hills and dales in shepherd-dress, making an
endless eclogue from life.

The interaction of these two characters is described by Sr. Madariaga's[1] clever phrase: the
quixotification of Sancho and the sanchification of
Don Quixote. Two human personalities in contact
attract each other, though they remain discrete. Don
Quixote is modified by Sancho, and Sancho is pulled
into the more powerful orbit of Don Quixote. In
this sense the introduction of Sancho Panza is the
most important moment of the novel; but it was

[1] S. de Madariaga, *Don Quixote*, Oxford, 1935, and *Guía del
Lector del Quijote*.

an afterthought. It was first the innkeeper of Puerto Lápiche who raised the question of securing a squire, as he strove to secure payment for the Knight's board and lodging. The squire was to serve chiefly as a purse-bearer. But the hint is taken up quite differently by the Knight:

'As there came to mind his host's advice about the necessary preparations he should carry, especially in money and shirts, he resolved to go home and get everything ready, including a squire; for he reckoned to take on a neighbouring peasant, who was poor and had children, but was well suited to the job of squire in chivalry.' (i. 4.)

The figure comes nearer (i. 7) when amplified as

'a neighbouring peasant, a decent fellow (if a poor man can be so described), but without much grey matter.'

Even so, Sancho merely abandons his wife and children, so that we have to wait until the Second Part for the rich comicity of Teresa Panza and Sanchica.

But though the phrase 'the quixotification of Sancho and the sanchification of Don Quixote' brilliantly expresses this aspect of the novel, it is in two ways less than the entire truth about either character. They both pursue their own orbits until they come to their radiant perihelion. No process of quixotification creates Teresa Panza, so as to give the sudden deepening of our regard for Sancho —cock of his own walk at least—which opens the Second Part. It is simply that we know more of Sancho. Because we know this much more, we are ready for him to play the leading role in the narrative, to contrive the adventures, propound wise saws, and govern an island with Solomonic rather than Quixotic genius. Nor is Sancho the cause why the hero's madness should follow the parabola from whole-hearted lunacy to the perplexed stages, even before it is overthrown altogether. Furthermore, quixotification and sanchification are not the cause but the consequence of their community of mind. Alonso Quijada el Bueno was as much a son of the soil as Sancho and has moments of earthy realism. It was Don Quixote who first propounded the philosophy of food, otherwise so nobly sustained by Sancho:

'for the toil and weight of arms cannot be endured without looking after the guts.' (i. 2.)

What persuaded Sancho to enter his service was not so much the island, but that the reward would come 'as quick as shifting straws'. Though he could not read, Sancho knew his ballads of chivalry to perfection. He was a master of proverbs, but it was Don Quixote who uttered the first one (i. 19), and it was he who advocated their use (i 21):

'I think, Sancho, that there is no untrue proverb, for they are all maxims drawn from experience itself, the mother of all knowledge.'

The basis of their common wit is the proverbial humour of countrymen; pure in Sancho, but curbed by reflection in Don Quixote.

We may take it that Alonso Quijada el Bueno was a frugal countryman, who ate his food in moderation and not without gusto. He liked field sports before the craze for fiction overwhelmed his liking. Shrewd and capable of pithy phrases, sententious

in the proverbial manner, he had curbed his rusti-
city by his good breeding, and through reading and
reflection he had generalized his knowledge. Sancho, lacking this education, perceived details with
the utmost clearness, but had no art to correlate
them. He could anchor his belief to some stubborn
particular, such as the blanketing in the First Part
and the bewitchment of Dulcinea in the Second, but
he could not controvert any general principle. The
power of generalizing belonged to Don Quixote and
was, by misuse, directed against the evidence of
particular facts. Herein lay his danger, and the
cause of his frequent dismays. But even in the first
five chapters we learn more of Don Quixote as a
man than this. His first emotion has nothing to do
with chivalry. It is the sudden rush of happiness
healthy persons feel when they escape from a routine:

'And so, not informing anyone of his intention or letting
anyone see him, one morning before daybreak—it was one
of the hot days of July—he fully armed himself, mounted
Rocinante, put on his ramshackle vizor, enarmed his targe,
picked up his lance, and issued from a courtyard postern
into the open country, mightily contented and excited to
find how easily he had made a beginning of his good intention.' (i. 2.)

It is with the same delight that he escaped from
the restrictions of the ducal palace in the Second
Part.

He reaches the Puerto Lápiche. The inn seems
to him a castle, with high-born ladies at its gate.
The humour seizes him to unload on them a flood
of fifteenth-century courtesies, which they naturally

fail to understand. No doubt this stately politeness was ludicrously misapplied to the two wantons, who were accustomed to hear the casual insults of gross men; but it not only amazed, it delighted them. They, too, became courteous and performed for Rocinante the services of gentlewomen in books of chivalry. Thus the innate courtesy of the Spanish countryman, so well known to all travellers, makes itself felt as an additional trait in Don Quixote's character. His modesty is shown by the patience with which he listens to the innkeeper, though himself undoubtedly a better authority on knightly usages. Once dubbed knight, he has no hesitation in laying down the laws of chivalry to Sancho or any other person. In his first adventure, which was that of Juan Haldudo and the boy Andresillo, he first gives evidence of his passion for fair play by reproving the stronger for an attack on the weaker; then he is piqued in his self-esteem; and finally he shows his own good faith by supposing an equal honesty in others. Thus, in these early chapters, before Sancho intervenes at all, Cervantes has begun to unfold a rare character, and to reveal its power to create its own surroundings. Don Quixote's spontaneous joy in freedom from constraint, his perfect courtesy, his sense of fair play, his seriousness and modesty, his personal dignity, these are qualities which have no necessary connexion with the profession of knight-errantry, though they are congruent thereto. Even in this little space he has become a lively figure; not a simulacrum, not a type.[1]

[1] The revelation of Don Quixote and Sancho Panza can be

The Knight of the Sorrowful Figure gave a verdict on his own case when he was about to mount Clavileño (ii. 41):

'If it all turns out the opposite of what I think, the glory of having attempted this exploit cannot be dimmed by any malice.'

Persons whom he trusted deceived him in that adventure. Little glory to them; no shame to him! In other cases he was deluded by conclusions drawn from his readings, and when he recovered sanity he damned Amadís and all his lineage. His judgement may have been at fault, but the resolves arising from that judgement were unimpeachable. He was really willing to fight against giants, spectres, lions, knights, and enchanters, though the things he so judged proved to be windmills, clerics, lackeys, butlers, and sheep. In the integrity of his righteousness he was undoubtedly 'the most chaste lover and valiant knight', not only in La Mancha, but in all his age.

But—he worked on a false apprehension of reality. It is the part of Sancho to work out the criticism of reality in all its multiple perplexity. The distinction is not as between true and false, for Don Quixote alone suffices for that. It is that true and false are so strangely blended in our experience that no one is at all times master of his reason. Sancho embodies common sense, but there are realities which escape common sense. What is immediately visible Sancho sees, but it is subsumed into a dream

followed in M. de Unamuno, *Vida de D. Quijote y de Sancho Panza*, Madrid, 1905.

for Don Quixote. But Sancho is liable to suffer the delusions of the senses, and he has no art of keeping alive past realities. The considerations and arguments of his master take his mind by storm, and he has to fight to retain the realism which seems connatural to his mind. He is driven into his last defences, of which the most serviceable was the blanketing. Whatever his master might say about goblins and spells, it was certain that ordinary men had held that blanket and that his master had been physically unable to intervene; and Sancho's sore ribs proved both affirmations. The blanketing was the irrefutable proof of his master's delusion.

But that was Sancho's last line; all others he was compelled to yield. In the affair of the windmills, he saw mills and Don Quixote saw giants. Don Quixote swept him aside by flat contradiction:

'It is evident, Don Quixote replied, that you are not *au fait* in the matter of adventures; they—are—giants.' (i. 8.)

At that moment the hero's lunacy was young and confident, as it was a few moments later when he lay sprawling on the ground.

'Quiet! friend Sancho, Don Quixote replied. Military affairs are more open than any others to continual reverses; the more so as I think, and it is the truth, that that sage Frestón, who robbed my room and books, has turned these giants into windmills.'

The first argument is a true proposition. The second contains the premiss 'I think, and so it is' (the *cogito ergo sum* of Descartes?), which Sancho was not fitted to dispute.

Adventures soon arise which are of a less simple type. In the great attack launched on the herds of merino sheep (i. 18) there was at first no visible enemy, but only tall pillars of dust. Don Quixote, looking with the mind's eye, reeled off figures and names; Sancho saw nothing in this to contradict. He saw the sheep at last, no doubt, but how could he know that they were sheep at the moment when his master had so clearly seen men-at-arms? A transformation might have been effected in the twinkling of an eye; and the only reason for doubting so was that the blanketing had been real. Mambrino or a barber was overthrown. The rank of the victim might be in dispute; but there were two relics of victory. Don Quixote had something which he declared to be an enchanted helmet, and Sancho had won stuffed saddle-bags. The helmet might look like a basin to Sancho (was Don Quixote's folly a little less confident than at the outset?), but 'what seems to you to be a barber's basin, seems to me to be Mambrino's helmet' (i. 25). How could Sancho, sure of his own truth about the saddle-bags, refuse to Don Quixote the truth that was his? Still more confusing was the affair of the fulling hammers. It was dark and no one really knew anything. The terrible hubbub kept both in terror all night long; and enchantment was a legitimate hypothesis. In the morning both recognized that the cause of the panic was the noise of fulling hammers. But fulling hammers are not a cause for terror, so whence came their night of fear?

The later half of the First Part reads like a preparation for the Second. Not only does Sancho begin to play pranks on his master, but outsiders intervene to deny the evidence of his senses. The conversation concerning the embassy to Dulcinea is the perfection of antithesis. There had actually been no meeting; but Sancho described in ever minuter detail a crude country lass about her chores, and Don Quixote as minutely substituted the corresponding attributes and gestures of a princess. The same event (though non-existent) was read one way by Sancho and another by Don Quixote, and there was no umpire to terminate the contention. (The case was reversed when they met Dulcinea on the road in the Second Part. Sancho affected to see a princess, and Don Quixote saw only a country lass on a donkey.) In later episodes an umpire was found in the Princess Micomicona, or the disguised Dorotea, who tipped the scale against Sancho's common sense, as the Duchess does in the Second Part. Therefore, Don Quixote's reasons prevail. Sancho detects the fraud and hurries to tell his master, and this is how it goes:

'Get up, sir, said Sancho, and see the fine message I have brought, and what we have to pay, and the queen converted into a private lady called Dorotea, with other things to amaze you if you get the hang of them.

'Nothing of the sort would amaze me, retorted Don Quixote; because, if you remember, the other time we were here I said that all that occurs here is matter of enchantment, so it would not be surprising if the same were so now.

'Yes, I could believe as much, Sancho replied, if my blanketing were also of that sort; but it was not; it occurred really and truly.' (i. 37.)

This palladium of the blanketing, however, could not

resist the express denial of Micomicona, supported
by all her friends. It is true that she took to kissing
in the corridors and other unregal things, and that
Sancho resumed his effort in the forty-eighth and
forty-ninth chapters; but common sense and the
evidence of one's eyes are ill matched against con-
certed reasons on the one side, and collusive testimony on the other.

The debate continues in the Second Part, which
belongs to Sancho. Here again is a crucial experiment and a conflict of witness. There are subsidiary
tests; and of these the most important was the
affair of Montesinos' cave. Cid Hamete left the
verdict open;

'for to think that Don Quixote would lie, being the truest
gentleman and noblest knight of his times, is impossible.
He would not tell a lie if he were shot at with arrows.'
(ii. 24.)

Besides there was the difficulty of fabricating so
elaborate a machine of fibs at a moment's notice.
On the other hand, what Don Quixote had to say
exceeded all reason. No oracle, whether wise mon-
key or enchanted head, would do more than say
that there was a mixture of truth and falsehood,
leaving each of the disputants to believe what he
liked. Don Quixote and Sancho mulled over the
difficulty, and for Sancho the only certainty was that
he had lied about the enchantment of Dulcinea.
There was nothing in that affair but what he had
done with his own perverse wits. Don Quixote had
no assurance on the point, for he came to doubt
whether there was a Dulcinea in the world (ii. 32);
but he was overborne by the general presupposition

of witchcraft, and the express testimony of the faithful, and unimaginative (or so he thought!), Sancho.
None the less, what he had seen was a raw country
lass. Then the Duchess intervenes. She puts it to
Sancho that his lie was not in the first but the second
degree, and that though fully intending a fraud, he
had been the unwitting accomplice of the truth.
Sancho's opposition crumbles:

'Believe me, Sancho, the high-kicking peasant was and
is Dulcinea del Toboso, enchanted like the mother that
bore her, and when we least think, we shall see her in her
own shape, and then Sancho will escape from the delusion
he lives in.

'All that may well be, said Sancho Panza. I am now
willing to believe what my master says he saw in the cave
of Montesinos. He says he saw Lady Dulcinea del Toboso
in the same dress and habit as I described when I enchanted
her for my own sweet pleasure. But it must all be quite
different, as Your Grace, madam, says, because it is not to
be imagined that my feeble wit would instantly fabricate so
cute a hoax, nor do I believe my master so mad as to believe
a thing out of all reason on so weak and slender a persuasion
as mine.' (ii. 33.)

Therefore, when it came to the whipping, Sancho
could not use the only rebutting reason, namely,
that Dulcinea was under no enchantment.

The episode was important to Don Quixote because it pegged his waning belief in enchanters and
enchantment. He had seen the commonplace face
of Sansón Carrasco in the downcast Knight of the
Mirrors, and the reputed seducer of the duenna's
daughter proved to be a vulgar lackey. A raw country girl on a donkey—it was Sancho who averred

she was Dulcinea. He could attend a puppet-show with phlegm, and take an inn for an inn. It was only the repeated insistence on a chivalresque motif that had power to inflame his mind, for it was rapidly approaching sanity. Sancho supposed that Clavileño was rushing through the air, but Don Quixote felt that he was on solid ground. All he did was rationally to infer their place in the heavens from the data Sancho's fears supplied. But there remained the case of the enchanted Dulcinea, supported by his own preconceptions against his eyes, and buttressed on the testimony of others. His folly had become exocentric.

It is the fundamental sanity of Don Quixote that is revealed in the numerous dissertations he makes *de omni re scibili*. He had spoken of Arms and Letters in the First Part; but in the Second he proves his wisdom in the fields of policy and public order, war, poetry, &c. These are his dissertations, and to them are to be added innumerable discussions with Sancho of the problem of truth and error. The author does not comply with his programme: 'Let Don Quixote attack and Sancho talk', for Don Quixote is slow to attack and talks more than Sancho. Sancho, indeed, has become the aggressive party. There is much give and take in their arguments. The First Part had excelled in action and the rich primal humour derived therefrom. The Second Part is an adventure of the mind, more subtly witty. It weakens when the fun degenerates into smart hoaxes at the ducal court, and dies in the last hurried chapters; but it is in the immortal conversations of the first seven, supplemented by the embassy to Teresa Panza, that the genius of Cervantes crowned itself with glory.

Here Sancho attains his majority. When we first encountered him we learned that he had a wife and children; but how little did we imagine what a wife ! She becomes a real person as the author's eye happens to catch her in focus, though still so dimly that he did not know whether she was called Juana or María Gutiérrez. Her name, of course— and now Cervantes sees her clearly in the opening of the Second Part—was neither Juana nor María, but Teresa Cascajo; and there was no surer disproof of the authenticity of Avellaneda's continuation than his ignorance of this elementary truth ! From a mere name in the First Part she becomes the exuberant creature of the Second (ii. 5, 50, 52). Similarly Sanchica was the bald 'children' of the First Part (i. 7), until she became the bewitchingly naïve creature of the Second (ii. 52). There seemed to be no end of the Panzas, and all enhance the glory of the one and only Sancho. In the Second Part he can turn a compliment, though he cannot remember one phrase of a letter in the First; he can utter real wisdom; he pours out proverbs like meal from a barrel, in a torrent of speech that outruns his own, not unnimble, thought. He accepts advice from his master, considers it, ignores it. He governs his island shrewdly, and resigns the government without regret. He is the same Sancho as in the First Part, but vastly more vivid and profound.

Of this change his master is fully aware. The original good dull-witted fellow has become, for Don Quixote, an exciting study:

'I should like Your Graces to know, on the other hand, that Sancho Panza is one of the most humorous squires that ever served a knight errant. Some of his naïveties are so acute, that it is a pleasing problem to determine whether he is a simpleton or a wit. His malice at times amounts to rascality, and his carelessness to thickheadedness. He doubts everything and believes everything. When I think he is rushing headlong into silliness, he comes out with some wisecracks that raise him sky-high.' (ii. 32.)

Sancho was aware of this and prided himself on his wit; if he did not always mean to be amusing, at least there was never any reason to complain of the result. But the conclusive proof of his advance in wisdom was his deep appreciation of his master. He knows he is mad, but not so very mad. As a 'sane madman' Don Quixote has ability enough for anything, including (which God forfend as of no profit to a married man like Sancho!) an archbishop. He is more than all this; more than a wage-payer and promiser of governments:

'for if I had been sensible, I would have left my master days ago. But it's just my luck and my ill-fortune. I cannot do it; I have to follow him; we are of the same village; I have eaten his bread; I really like him; he is grateful; he gave me his own colts, and above all I am trusty; and so we cannot part any more than the handle and the hoe. If Your Highmindedness doesn't want to give me the promised governorship,—well, God made me from less, and perhaps not giving it will be of advantage to my conscience. Though I am a simpleton I understand the meaning of the proverb that "no good came of the ant's wings", and perhaps Squire Sancho will get quicker into heaven than Governor Sancho.' (ii. 33.)

THE MEANING OF *DON QUIXOTE*

Esta vuestra historia no mira a más que a deshacer la autoridad y cabida que en el mundo y en el vulgo tienen los libros de caballerías.

THE late Miguel de Unamuno[1] would not even treat of the Scrutiny, saying that it concerns books, not life. In this he made an antithesis as old as Thucydides and strangely attractive to men of letters, who, despite their *métier*, like to pretend that words and deeds are poles apart. In this, as in the poets' claim to artless inspiration, they are disingenuous. Deeds are the outward garments of words, though there are also words which are not clothed in deeds. Nothing, however trivial or sublime, arises save from a root of words, and when words are garnered and multiplied in a book they have a life more vigorous than the generations. Of the thirteen million contemporaries of Cervantes in Spain, how many now have the life that radiates in the book? The book is even in a sense superior to the author. The Cervantes of the *Galatea* exerts little more interest than the forgotten grandee; but *Don Quixote* reveals him as more than human. His biography is subordinate to his writings.

However, the difficulty which Unamuno alleged in the single chapter has been felt by other critics in all the work. They are reluctant to believe that Cervantes' purpose was what he himself repeatedly averred, and his friend José de Valdivielso confirmed: to put down the credit that books of chivalry had gained in unbalanced minds. Don Quixote on

[1] *Vida de Don Quixote y de Sancho,* Madrid, 1905.

his death-bed, in the full enjoyment of his faculties, solemnly anathematized the *Amadís* cycle; but the ironist, like the liar, can hardly win belief even when speaking the truth. It is alleged that these intentions may only be another example of Cervantes' sardonic wit; that the literature of chivalry was already dead and only awaited interment; that a bookish target was too petty for so great a projectile; that the lover of chivalry was not the man to destroy it; that his grave teaching is a sign to look for some transcendental purpose. Yet no one of these considerations is entirely convincing. It is true that new books of chivalry were rarely issued in the third quarter of the sixteenth century, but their authority had not yet followed the same declining curve. Their interminable adventures still provided serial reading for the inns and country houses of Spain. The village priest, though a graduate of Sigüenza, was not slower than the Knight to take up the comparison of Amadís and Palmerín, and the surgeon-barber had a third favourite. In the fields at harvest-time someone read these books to the reapers; the furibund slashes delighted the innkeeper till he forgot to scold his wife, his serving-wench warmed herself in the imagined embraces of a knight beneath the orange-tree, and his daughter languished for the absent lover. So eminent a dignitary as a Canon of Toledo had a scheme for a more perfect novel, and the country gentleman who had no such books must have been an exception. Undergraduates, travelling merchants, bandits, dukes, and boors fall into the chivalresque dialect as soon as they hear it, until at length the Manchegan is borne up on the words and suggestions of others, rather than by his own folly. To take two conclusive examples which do not depend, like the above, on the Cervantine text: chivalrous adventure suggested to the child Teresa the notion of a sally to seek martyrdom among the Moors, and Ignacio de Loyola created for the defence of Holy Church a godly chivalry, starting from the vigil of Montserrat.

The truth is that Cervantes esteemed his *métier* more highly than his critics have done. He was a maker of books of honest entertainment, and it was important to him that only the best of such books should be publicly received. They were a necessity in the republic, like avenues and pleasant vistas. The bow must not always be bent; toil must be relieved by pleasure. But the pleasure should be elevating and instructive, and it was a poignant anxiety of the maker of honest entertainment that nothing should sully his art. Harm, both moral and aesthetic, could be done by the abuse of chivalry, the exemplary instance being the Manchegan. Continuous reading of fiction had enveloped his mind in the 'murky shades of ignorance', and made him sally forth to put into practice feats and customs which had no place in actual life. In doing so, he overestimated his strength and that of his skinny beast, and he suffered continual overthrow. What was plain and palpable before his eyes he judged to be strange and romantic. This evil was wrought by books of chivalry, and there was an evil of lascivious amorousness which contemporary clerics condemned, though with only lukewarm support from Cervantes; for Cervantes was always one to pardon

sins to lovers. He is careful, however, to make Don
Quixote the chastest as well as the bravest cavalier
seen for many a day in La Mancha.

Sickness of wit was grave enough, but the fault
of art touched Cervantes more closely; for books
of chivalry lacked all verisimilitude. It is the maker
of books who speaks at this point (i. 47), demand-
ing of the empty air, with exasperation, what makes
best-sellers of books devoid of reasonable foundation, serious purpose, orderly arrangement, or grace
of style. What beauty, what pleasure is there in
being told that a boy of sixteen chops into slices a
giant as big as a tower, and singly vanquishes a
million foes? What are we to say to queens and
empresses who drop so casually into the arms of
unknown knights? What of the towers that sail like
ships, and the prodigious leaps from Lombardy to
Cathay? What of the disorder of the narrative, in
which episodes lie jumbled as if in a sack, without
beginning, middle, or end? The style is crude, the
loves lascivious, the battles tedious, and the voyages
absurd; in short, such works are harmful to the
republic, and should be banished and destroyed.
But—these were the best-sellers of the day, to the
not inconsiderable chagrin of the greatest of Spanish
novelists who, at the advanced age of fifty-eight,
still failed to attract the public notice. He could
only suppose that the public needed the protection
of some inquisition or (in modern terms) of sound
criticism which would signalize the good and un-
mask the bad.

Cervantes was, however, far too good a book-maker
not to recognize success when he saw it. Modern

ingenuity has suggested that there can be unliterary
successes, 'bookless books' as the Greeks would
have said, and that this class may be made to embrace
the majority of best-sellers; but Mr. C. S. Lewis
has shown that this view is an illusion. The bad
book succeeds, if it does, by reason of some merit,
however slight; and Cervantes, following Pliny,
remarked that 'there is no book so bad as not to be
good in parts' (ii. 3). These long romances served
very well to relieve the tedium of pages idling in
baronial corridors, and of country householders
in long evenings. Many as they were, they were
still not numerous in comparison with the supply of
our day, so that it was a convenience that one book
should spread over many nights. Read piecemeal,
the incongruity of the parts may have seemed less
blatant, provided the immediate chapter gave good
entertainment. The appeal was to the romantic
susceptibilities of people leading dull lives. It was
a literature of escape, in which the man of routine
could achieve dazzling victories, the snub-nosed
wench be loved, and the inexperienced girl have a
foretaste of the sweets of elegant courtship. Cervantes saw these effects in others because he felt
them in himself. As a practical novelist rather than
a critic, he felt that their authority could be under-
mined, not by fulminations, but by the evidence of
something better.

It is this better thing that the Canon of Toledo
described in a famous passage (i. 47). The genre
itself was not evil. Mindful of the quarrel raging
in Italy about the *romanzo* and the *epos*, Cervantes
reveals himself as the champion of the new style.

It gave space for the free exercise of the pen in describing battles, storms, encounters, and shipwrecks; in portraying the perfect captain, prudent, eloquent, mature in counsel, swift in act, enduring, valiant. A world of human beings was ready to crowd the pages: lovely ladies, Christian leaders, uncouth barbarians, courteous princes and loyal vassals. The riches of the mind would be revealed in episodes of astrology, cosmography, music, statecraft. The passions awaited incarnation in bodies worthy of Virgil and Homer's heroes. A pleasant style and ingenious originality, salted with variety and joined with judgement, would lead to the union of pleasure and instruction through the whole gamut of tones: tragic, comic, epic, lyrical. In short, the qualities and actions that go to make a complete man would be wedded to the delights of poetry and oratory, making, though in prose, a veritable epos.

Scholars have recognized in these words the programme of *Persiles and Sigismunda*, the novel that was to outclass Heliodorus, whereas *Don Quixote* was the child of a gloomy prison. It is undeniable that Cervantes miscalculated; the overwhelming success of *Don Quixote*, sharing some of these virtues with others undeclared, made it the 'best of chivalrous novels'. In it we find the merits of its predecessors combined with a new realism, a loftier idealism, a wider experience of life, and a more reflective judgement. Even in the wildest among them there had been a mustard-seed of truth, though under a figure; but truth was bound to *Don Quixote* by many mighty cords.

In all this Cervantes was following in the wake of the great Ariosto, his kinsman in sympathy and form. *Don Quixote* is formally unlike the *Orlando Furioso* almost only by the fact of its being written in prose. It shows the same ironical sympathy for an ideal judged impossible, and flows with a like exuberance of invention. But Ariosto took refuge in the sheer ingenuity and loveliness of his dream, whereas Cervantes posed the weighty question of truth. He showed lofty motives and acts clashing against a world of heartless wit and picaresque roguery, and by so doing he revealed the double character of his age—rusty iron under brave plumes. His own mind, the mind of his hero, soared towards a perfection which seemed possible in reason and by the light of Nature; but his hero was cast down by irrefutable facts, and he himself, instead of being maintained (as French travellers expected) in the Prytanaeum, was at the advanced age of sixty-eight 'old, a soldier, a gentleman, and poor'.

This double meaning of *Don Quixote*, which raises it above all other works of the age save *Hamlet*, has been annexed by Spanish critics to the two planes of the Golden Age : the upward, optimistic thrust of Erasmian humanism, and the downward, hypocritical plunge of the Tridentine Counter-Reformation.[1] The parallel is ingenious, but should not be pressed too far. *Don Quixote* remains a work of the imagination, with no other ostensible purpose than to discredit a particular literary genre. If it is a picture of an age, it is not a tract for the times. That the young Cervantes came under strong Erasmian

[1] A. Castro, *El Pensamiento de Cervantes*, Madrid, 1925.

influence has been sufficiently determined. He was an optimist by conviction. Even *in articulo mortis* he writes to say that there are fine books ready to be completed by his pen. But he remained a lay spirit throughout his life; and if Tridentine precepts and national reverses forced him to abate some hopes, he met disasters with innate courage. His real instructor was not Trent nor the Armada, but the disorder of his own life. After thirty years of literary struggle he had no reputation in 1605; and he was hopelessly entangled by his failure as a bureaucrat. Ten years later his fame was greater than that of any writer but Lope de Vega, but he was considered a humorist rather than an artist; he had fame of a sort, but he was 'old, a soldier, a gentleman, and poor'. If he wished to take a seat among the poets, there was none to spare, and Apollo bade him fold his cloak and sit on it, not troubling to notice that he had none. For the disconcert of the world (as Camões had it) he needed no other testimony than his own troubled life.

Nevertheless Cervantes remains undefeatably on the side of the angels. His hero follows a career of triumph, and not merely in his own mind. He is a victor because he believes himself victorious. But he is a victor also because his living will moulds the environment to his own pattern. Courtesans and inns become damosels and castles; no thrill of heroic combat is lacking to the fight with the Biscayan; lions are vanquished. He transformed the life of his village, so that the priest masqueraded as a distressed damsel, the barber lost his beard, and Sansón Carrasco became a knight in enchanted armour. He transformed the routine of a ducal castle, making its life revolve round his prowess, so that Sancho really gained his island. He was acclaimed by all who met him, and entered Barcelona with an ovation. This was all real in a way, and it was all the real life that Don Quixote—a representative figure for all mortals—really enjoyed. Then came defeat, truth, death: three synonyms.

The exaltation of this sadly heroic figure came from the very irony in which it was conceived. Even in the first prologue we learn that he was the chastest and most valiant of the Manchegan knights; and virtue is not diminished by limitations of space. Mad as a hatter on one point, he discourses with exemplary wisdom on many others, and his dissertations are an astonishment to Sancho and an education for all he meets. He makes country gentlemen, riotous bloods, moon-struck boys, and idle grandees think about public service, the ends of culture, the essentials of virtue. He seeks to perform a greathearted public service which no one is willing to take up:

'A gallant knight is a fine thing for his king to see in the middle of a great square, delivering a happy lance-thrust into a wild bull; and a knight in splendid armour is a fine sight as he passes the drapery before the ladies in joyful jousts, and a fine sight are all those knights who, in military exercises or others like them, amuse and delight and (so to say) confer honour on the courts of their princes; but far finer above all these is a knight errant in search of perilous adventures in deserts, wastes, crossways, woods and mountains, with the firm intention of finding a happy and fortunate issue, for the mere sake of glorious and durable fame. Far finer, I say, is a knight errant succouring a widow on a heath than a courtier flirting with a girl in the city. Every knight has his special exercises; let the courtier wait on the ladies, give dignity to the court with his liveries, maintain poor gentlemen with the splendid service of his table; let him arrange jousts, maintain tourneys, and show himself to be grand, liberal, magnificent, and especially a good Christian; in this way he will perform his essential obligations. But let the knight errant seek the corners of the world, plunge into most intricate labyrinths, constantly attempt the impossible, suffer the burning rays of the midsummer sun on open and deserted plains, and suffer the cruel unkindness of wintry winds and frosts. No lion should frighten him nor goblin nor sprite; to seek trials and attack monsters and overcome them all are his true and principal exercises.' (ii. 17.)

And, turning to Sancho, he added:

'What do you think, Sancho? Are there enchantments to prevail against true valour? Enchanters may well deprive me of luck, but by no means of strength and courage.'

It was true that this business of succouring the widow and the orphan had rather gone out of fashion. The dukes, barbers, and innkeepers had more urgent trifles to attend to. Yet if the meaning of the novel were to be pressed into a word, that word would be Justice. The most absolute, unbending justice is Don Quixote's guiding star: 'to crush force and succour and aid the wretched' (i. 22). This Virgilian principle is announced in the episode of the galley-slaves, whom the Knight freed on the ground that no one should be constrained against his own will. It was not a principle to be applied to a singularly sinful world, and it led to ingratitude and lapidation. His impartiality is absolute: after procuring Andresillo's liberation on a protest of innocence he as freely accepts Juan Haldudo's promise not to be vindictive; and he was deluded on both counts. But he had maintained a standard; and this standard he urged, with complete reasonableness, against the Catalan bandit Roque Guinart, urging him to use the same courage and resource in the service of good. Justice attributes to each man that which is his due, and is the corner-stone of the State. It was the stone which the visionary Manchegan sought to lay in the idle, ostentatious, privileged, and unequal Spain of Philip III. Facts proved him wrong, but who was the better for the facts?

It would seem that *Don Quixote* is a book to be read at least twice in a lifetime. It is a book for boys or young men, who enjoy its riotous fun without a second thought. For them it is swift, joyous, ridiculous, extravagant. It must be taken up later when middle life has brought a store of experience. The reader of mature age knows that hopes are dimmed and die, that cherished achievements have been ignored, and (what is more bitter) that unworthy things have been praised. The mood is not of defeat, but of frustration. For such *Don Quixote* is real, tragic, strong, triumphant. Both views are true, but the second is more consoling. We see that the will is better than the deed and overcomes dead, hostile reality. The universe neither loves nor hates us, as we dash our puny fists against its implacable strength. Like grass-seed under a stone we are most likely to be smothered; but it is the grass-seed that has the principle of life, and in time tender blades will dislodge the inert obstacle. In the last analysis, all life is stronger than all death. Men also thrust against the universe and thrust in vain; but it is their energy and purpose that signify. We have power to create our own microcosm, and in relation to us the universe is a construction of our own minds. Anything less, for us as for Don Quixote, is defeat and death; but so long as we live, we triumph.

THE HERO AS PEDANT

— ¿ *Reglas quies poner a amor ?*
— *La razón puede ponellas.*

THE message of *Don Quixote* will differ from reader
to reader. What to some seems an affirmation
of Humanism, to others will seem the spirit of the
Counter-Reformation; to some the work is high
tragedy, to others comedy. It was accepted with
hilarity on its first issue, and for many years it was
not accorded the rank of a work of art. First
seriously esteemed in England, it was first idolized
in Germany, and the diverse appreciations of generations have made a direct approach almost impossible. One is bound to entertain some preconceived
opinion of a work universally famous. The experience of reading it changes such opinions, but it
is a joint product of the author's language and
the reader's outlook on life. *Don Quixote* is not
unique in this respect, which is rather one of the
marks of greatness in literature. The great work
so far transcends its origin as to become encrusted
with many strata of meaning, and to provoke a
fresh response at every reading.

In a more limited sense, however, no man took
more care to be explicit than Cervantes.[1] He is a
mighty pedant, with rules for everything, even for
falling in love. Many of the greatest writers have
been teachers, but few have given lessons in so many
subjects as our author, who believed in the reasonableness of Nature, and therefore the teachability
of all good things. It is true that he writes with

[1] A. Castro, *El Pensamiento de Cervantes*, Madrid, 1925.

irony, but this disturbing effect has been discounted by Dr. Castro in an ingenious manner. Cervantes is addicted to short dogmatic statements on a variety of subjects. Once it is granted that his formation was Erasmian, these statements can be identified with those of Erasmus or his Spanish followers, and whenever they coincide we may be sure that Cervantes speaks seriously. His *obiter dicta* may thus be rearranged on a more systematic plan, and their mutual conformity observed. What emerges is a body of doctrine relying on the same guiding principles, which are a proof that this author, so long suspected of 'warbling his native woodnotes wild', had the disposition, if not the training, of a moral and social philosopher.

His views may be summarized briefly in these pages, but for a fuller statement the reader should consult Dr. Castro's masterly book. It is necessary to appreciate the temper of the man who devoted so much of his literary effort to exemplary fiction, since it was this temper which led to his greatest achievement. This is not to say that the saving grace of *Don Quixote* is its doctrinal aspect, but it is to recognize that the desire to correct an error was a chief cause of its beginning.

The foundation of Cervantes' doctrine is his view of Nature. Nature is entirely perfect and entirely reasonable. Nature is the vice-gerent of God, but with a strictly defined sphere of action; for she may proceed only according to reason, whereas God may interrupt brusquely the course of Nature. Here lies miracle. Miracles must be accepted as facts since they are supported both by Scripture and by modern testimonies. Some of those concerning St. Teresa, for instance, have this support, and Cervantes argues that her unsupported miracles may be accepted by analogy. It is the same with Cristóbal de Lugo. His assumption of the sins of another was supported by the express evidence of ecclesiastics, and Cervantes' rubrics call attention to this weight of evidence for that which, within natural limits, it might be difficult to credit. But as facts miracles are incalculable, and should normally be ignored. They would lack verisimilitude by their very definition, and they are therefore not proper subjects for the literature of entertainment, whose charm consists in the imitation of Nature. By the same process of argument this literature will not make much use of the divine, since the leading sign of divine intervention is an interruption of the laws of Nature. A profoundly lay spirit thus rules in Cervantes' writings, and marks him off from the greater number of his contemporaries, who are only too prompt to bring the god in his machine. He has almost entirely excluded religious topics from his purview, and in his reliance on the universal and human he speaks of things that all men understand. His work stands the test of age and change of scene the better for this restriction of range; his genius is universal, because humane.

Nature, being reasonable, can be taught and known. She is simple, because the simple is fundamental. An educated common sense can grasp her main principles, and lead to the happy life through conformity with Nature. Religion, for instance, is a question of the pure soul and the sincere heart, as the Numantine priests declare, beside which an elaborate ritual of sacrifice is of little consequence. But this is a line which Cervantes does not follow; Juan de Valdés had followed it in his religious tractates, which are interesting suggestions of a might-have-been in Spanish religious history. It is quite likely that Cervantes would not have travelled so far as Valdés, since he was more disposed, on common-sense grounds, to accept the guidance of experts. It is a point to which we shall have to return.

The life according to Nature is harmonious; faults and errors are dissonant.

> The man of sense is concordance,
> engendered by ability,
> the silly soul disparity,
> incapable of consonance.

The tests of harmony and dissonance reveal the rights and wrongs of human conduct. To these particular applications Nature stands as a universal, and this antithesis corresponds in literature to the difference between poetry and history. History relies on the truth of each and all of its particulars, but poetry rises superior to this niggling accuracy because it attains the universals, its method being verisimilitude.

Verisimilitude produces a number of illuminating pictures of Nature, among which the myth of the Golden Age and the pastoral convention are most attractive. These shepherds live according to Nature in no particular sense, since the particular country-side has the grossness which is described in *The Dogs' Colloquy*. The truth of the pastoral is a poetic or universal truth, and it represents under human symbols the perfection of natural simplicity. The same poetic truth is to be seen in the myth of the Golden Age, and it is the object and ambition of the good knight errant to restore, so far as may be, this state of pristine happiness.

'Happy the age and happy those centuries [cries Don Quixote] which the ancients called golden. Not because gold, so highly prized in this our time, was then obtained without any toil, but because those who then lived did not know the two words *tuum* and *meum*. In that holy age all things were in common. To gain his ordinary sustenance no one needed to take more trouble than to raise his hand and pick acorns from the sturdy oaks, which so liberally offered their sweet and savoury fruit. Clear streams and running rivers offered them tasty transparent water in abundance. The wise and busy bees formed their republics in the crannies of rocks and hollows of trees, and offered gratis to every hand the fertile crop of their sweet labour. Cork-trees shed with artless courtesy their broad light bark, wherewith a beginning was made on the roofs of houses upon a frame of supporting stakes, without other object than protection against the inclemency of heaven. All was peace, all friendship, all concord. At that date the heavy iron of the curved plough had not ventured to open or visit the pitiful bowels of our first mother; for she offered without force from all parts of her broad and fertile bosom enough to satisfy, sustain and delight the children who then possessed her. It was then that the simple, lovely girls rambled from valley to valley and hillock to hillock, in their virginal integrity, with no more clothes than those needed honestly to cover that which honesty seeks and has always sought to cover. They did not wear the gauds now used, made costly by Tyrian purple and tortured silk; they were adorned with plaits of burdock and ivy leaves, which were perhaps as elegantly decorative as the strange

new inventions that the curiosity of triflers has revealed to
our ladies of the court. In that age the loving fancies of the
heart were plainly and simply got by rote, just as the heart
conceived them, without artificial circumlocution to heighten
their effect. No fraud, trickery or malice was commingled
with the plain truth. Justice kept its bounds, not disturbed
or offended by favour and interest, which now so grievously
diminish, perturb and persecute justice. Arbitrary dealings
had not taken their seat in the judge's brain, since there was
nothing and nobody to be judged. Damsels went with their
honesty everywhere, as I have said, alone and unaccompanied,
without fear of injury from the forwardness and wanton intentions of others; their loss of virginity came from their own
pleasure and will. But in this detestable age of ours, no
virgin is secure, though she be hidden and enclosed in a new
Cretan labyrinth; since here, through the crannies or by the
air, with accursedly industrious assiduity, the amorous pestilence comes to them and makes them cast away all their
self-respect. To secure them, as time rolled on and malice
increased, the order of knights errant was instituted, to defend damsels, protect widows, succour the orphan and the
needy.' (i. 11.)

Hence the strong attraction felt by Cervantes for
the *Galatea* which portrays this perfection, and for
novels of chivalry which seek its restoration. Pristine simplicity also made commendable those proverbs which were 'maxims drawn from experience
itself, the mother of all knowledge', and those racy
and rustic turns of speech which were free from
the corrupting influence of fashion. In short, the
'people' looms behind these ideas as the idealized
exponent of natural simplicity, and the 'noble savage'
is not far to seek.

This simplicity, being based on reason, might be

attained through education. The educational process
was a kind of recovery of former virtue, since the
theory of corruption applied not only to morals but
to intellectual things. In the realm of language these
theories produced many cross-currents. The speech
of peasants and proverbs were standards of spontaneous simplicity, but Augustan Latin was another.
The modern representatives of Latin were the product of greater or less corruption, so that the recovery of Latin words and usages was a return to
Nature. The care of style was also a means to the
same end, so that the path to Nature lay through
Art. In the early years of the sixteenth century
Juan de Valdés claimed to write as he spoke and
Garcilaso de la Vega required only that affectation
be avoided. They both used the Spanish language
as persons born in Toledo and brought up at the
Court; that is to say, what seemed natural to them
was the choice and purified speech of the upper
classes. This need for selection was stressed by Fray
Luis de León, who added that the weight of words
and even their letters should be taken into account.
It was a poet's demand. In his most exalted passages
this measurement leads to the inclusion of hendeca-
syllables and heptasyllables in considerable numbers. At about the same time Cervantes proposed
for style four characteristic marks: ease, sweetness,
gravity, eloquence. The second pair of qualities
considerably modified the first, and the Cervantine
prose paragraph stands at a distant remove from
the brief sententiousness of the proverb. In his great
period, indeed, the two styles are brought to give a
lively contrast; Don Quixote's sonorous eloquence

and the proverbial sententiousness of Sancho Panza.
On behalf of poetry Fernando de Herrera demanded
a still wider range of qualities. His principal effort
was to dignify and ennoble the language by discreetly incorporating the resources of Latin under
the guidance of Italian mentors. The numerous
neologisms and latinisms of his style are evidence
of an attempt to escape the normal prosaic level.
In the major poems of Góngora Herrera's struggle
to eject the normal was pursued without his caution,
so that the sense is not to be attained through reliance on the common tongue. Antithesis, oxymoron,
abstract for concrete, concrete for abstract, classical
allusion, petrified metaphor, hyperbaton, parenthe-
sis—these were the resources of Góngora's style,
which would none the less claim to be sweet, easy,
and natural. It will be seen that Cervantes occupies
the point of equilibrium in this development from
the simple to the artificial.

The same demand for art is made by Cervantes of
all spheres of activity. He recognizes the existence
of native Solomonic wit in the Barataria episode and
the *Election of the Provosts of Daganzo*, since it is
possible to state the qualities of good government
in simple words. But at the same time he condemns
Sancho for ignorance of the art of government,
though Don Quixote had done his best to instruct
him. Sancho maintains that 'though I don't know
my ABC, it is enough to keep the *Christus* in memory
to be a good governor', but Don Quixote and his
maker would have submitted every candidate to a
severe test in arms and letters. No one believed in
the examination system so fervently as Cervantes!

In the same way the art of war was subject to rules, of which he gives some inkling in the *Numantia* and *The gallant Spaniard*, and there is an art of being an actor which is detailed in *Pedro de Urdemalas*. The actor must have a good memory, ready utterance, elegant appearance, height, unaffected gestures; he must not intone his words, but use a studied negligence, accompanied by good sense and diligence; he must add interest to his lines and bring to life a dead text;

> the expression he puts on,
> on each auditor should show;
> if the actor makes it so,
> then I call him champion.

The applications of this art to achieve Nature are too numerous to be detailed in this brief statement, but we must dwell on one curious aspect. In his treatment of love and honour Cervantes stands apart from all his contemporaries, since he differs from them in first principles. Love is the 'marriage of true minds', based on harmony and interrupted by dissonance. He transcribed the doctrine of the Neoplatonists in his *Galatea*, but the instances created by his own fancy are more significant. The sacrament confirms such a marriage, but is not an essential; and Cervantes frequently dispenses with a wedding. Neither the sacrament nor the social order can plead for maintaining a marriage which has ignored the requirement of compatibility.

'The seventy-year old who marries a girl of fifteen either is bereft of understanding or is anxious to reach the other world as soon as possible.' (*The jealous old Man.*)

In short, there is no remedy for an unnatural marriage, and the blame in such cases lies not with the unfaithful party but with the party who urged it in contempt of reason. In *The jealous Extremaduran* the lady is specifically excused in the older text, and in all cases her actions are shown to be the inevitable consequences of her husband's conduct. If there is desertion, then let the husband thank heaven he is rid of a knave. If the fortress of matrimony has been successfully assaulted, then let discretion be practised, together with dissimulation. The stories of *Tricked into Marriage* and *The Talaveran Wanton* support the former moral, and *The Call of the Blood* has to do with the concealment of shame. It is in keeping with this sentiment that Cervantes should treat so humanely the outcasts of the social system, so that through her 'beauty and discretion' the Esperanza of *The feigned Aunt* should reach a happy settlement. Nothing could be farther from the notion of an indissoluble sacrament than this identification of marriage with compatibility of temperament; nothing less like the savage code of honour which, exemplified by the comedies of the day, demanded that all matrimonial failings should be wiped out in blood, secretly, savagely, and totally.

Error is, therefore, dissonance in Nature. Cervantes admits that it is not always easy to perceive the simple truth which our senses are wont to misconstrue. We may wilfully contravene her behests, as in the case of disparate marriages, but we may also suffer from illusion. In the more difficult cases, indeed, truth may be twofold and relative. There is universal truth which differs from particular truths,

and there are differences of opinion, such as that
which divided Don Quixote from Sancho in the
matter of Mambrino's helmet. To the one it
seemed a helmet, to the other a barber's basin; and
there was no arbitrament. Further, between admitted principles and their applications there is room
for error, as in the case of medicine and astrology.
Nature has healing resources, but doctors slay like
the ancient Britons, on foot and in chariots. The
fundamental tenet of astrology is the oneness of the
universe and therefore the significant interrelation
of all its parts, but individual prognostications are
usually erroneous. In such a case Cervantes blames
not the science, about which he remains an agnostic,
but the practitioner:

> 'Tis a science I condemn
> not qua science, but because
> fools rush in, and study's laws
> and experience contemn.

Meanwhile astrology and even witchcraft are tools
of the novelist for what they possess of verisimilitude.

It is this business of entertainment which must
be kept firmly in mind when discussing Cervantes'
thought. It is true that he reflected on many phases
of experience and that his reflections take shape in a
certain pattern; but they occur only as *obiter dicta*
in a setting of fiction, and they frequently serve
limited purposes. In *The Call of the Blood*, for instance, a lady has been violated and in the denouement she achieves honourable wedlock. It was
convenient that this climax should be brief and
striking. Cervantes reduces the marriage ceremony
to a brief exchange of promises before witnesses,

'without the just and holy steps and precautions now in use'. Do such words, in their context, conceal a barb directed against the Tridentine insistence on the sacrament of marriage? Surely not; they cover only a fiction-writer's convenience. They do fit into a theory of marriage as consonance of two minds, and such a theory takes no account of sacramental sanction. As in his aversion from the miraculous, there were lines in Cervantine thought which, if produced, might have pierced Catholic orthodoxy; but they were not so prolonged by Cervantes, nor did contemporary licencers see in his work anything obnoxious to the faith. There were regions into which he did not care to enter; provinces that belonged to other orders of expert opinion. Like his own Mauricio, Cervantes accepted the views which he perceived to be consonant with reason; where he could not reasonably account for dogma, he conformed, since even a reluctant assent did less harm than open and head-strong rebellion. This suppression of private judgement he was wont to call hypocrisy, asserting that

now and then dissimulation pays.

Dr. Castro has seen in his words evidence of a stifled rejection of the official creed; a deep-seated hypocrisy that caused him covertly to rail, while making, with his tongue in his cheek, loud professions of orthodoxy. Had Cervantes intended to attack contemporary Catholicism I cannot but feel that the hero of Lepanto would have taken a more open course. It is not impossible to admit his protestation of orthodoxy as true of his intentions, though his lay conception of the world might have given an unorthodox picture. Cervantes was not systematic, since he was neither a theologian nor a philosopher, but a maker of honest entertainment, whose work was richer because of its attitude to life, which applied the same tests to many sorts of experience, but without necessary consistency or transcendental intent.

OCEAN OF STORY

El último sueño romántico de Cervantes.

THE last phase was a passionate love of story-telling. Cervantes, though he kept enough in hand to promise a new *Decameron* under the title of *Weeks in the Garden*, packed a score of short stories and anecdotes into an envelope of romantic adventure, and thus made his 'great *Persiles*'. Few books have ever been announced with more confidence by an author. In the preliminaries of the Second Part of *Don Quixote*, the book being then about four months from completion, he announced that it was to be 'either the worst or the best composed in our language, that is, of books of entertainment; and I say I regret having said "the worst", because in my friends' opinion it will attain the extreme of possible goodness'. Two years earlier he had said that it was a work which 'dares to compete with Heliodorus'. It was to fulfil a programme announced as early as the first part of *Don Quixote* (i. 47), where the Canon of Toledo describes the perfect novel.

'In spite of all the criticisms levied against such books, he found one good thing in them, namely, the opportunity they offered for a good brain to display itself, with a large and spacious field wherein the pen could run without any sort of hindrance. One could describe shipwrecks, storms, duels and battles, while depicting a valiant captain with all the qualities needed, as he shows foresight in divining his enemy's ruses, and an orator's eloquence when persuading or dissuading his soldiers, being prompt in decision and as courageous in awaiting attack as in making it. The author can paint a lamentable tragedy or some unexpectedly cheerful occurrence; a lovely, honest, discreet, circumspect lady; a valiant and courteous Christian gentleman; a farouche barbarian; a courtly, valiant and tactful prince; forming a picture of goodness and loyalty in vassals and of greatness and munificence in lords. He can display his knowledge of astrology, cosmography, music, statecraft, and he might even, if he wished, appear as a necromancer. He can put on view Ulysses' wiles, Aeneas' piety, Achilles' valour, Hector's ill-fortune, Sinon's treason, Euryalus' friendship, Alexander's liberality, Caesar's bravery, Trajan's clemency and truthfulness, Zopyrus' faithfulness, Cato's prudence, and in short all those actions that make perfect a hero, whether he concentrate them in an individual or distribute them among many. If this be carried out in a pleasant style and with ingenious inventiveness, steering as closely as possible to the truth, our author would no doubt compose a cloth woven from various lovely threads. Once completed, it would be so perfectly beautiful as to attain the best end proposed for literature, that is, as I have said, to join doctrine to pleasure. The free style of such books allows the author to exploit the epic, lyric, tragic, and comic veins, with all the qualities included in the sweetly pleasing sciences of poetry and oratory; for the Epos can be written as well in prose as in verse.'

It has been pointed out[1] that this description corresponds to the praise Alonso López (called El Pinciano) gave to Heliodorus in his dialogues of *Ancient Poetic Philosophy* in 1596. For that critic Virgil and Homer were two figures in a triad which included the Greek novelist, and he specially praised the incognito of the hero and heroine. It is clear that Cervantes' mind was already eager to rival the unapproachable standard of his art as novelist,

[1] A. Castro, *El Pensamiento de Cervantes,* Madrid, 1925, p. 44.

though it happens that he succeeded not in the *Persiles* but in the *Quixote*. The elevation and variety which he sought to attain were present in *Don Quixote* in the strictly human measure permitted to the novelist, and the attempt to gild the lily in his later work proved his undoing. It suffers indeed from what might be called the exemplary fallacy. The portrait of the perfect prince fails to excite admiration because it is monotonous. Persiles and Sigismunda arouse no interest in themselves or their adventures, and the parade of a rather transparent incognito is merely irritating. The author himself must have tired of their perfection, since he allows them little space in his best chapters, and botches the end of the book to get them married and put away. Still, no doubt, the experiment had to be made to be believed. The epic poets of the age were striving to express the perfect character, and a novelist who believed in the prose epos was bound to test his theory. Had he lived longer he might have agreed that the novel, like tragedy, needs the saving human touch of imperfection.

The correspondence between Cervantes and Heliodorus may be worked out to any desired number of decimals. Invention required that the plot should be his own, and the principle of imitation required that it should run parallel with the admired model. The incognito of the hero and heroine in each book has a double source: the desire to avoid unwelcome attentions from corsair princes, and convenience in making together a religious pilgrimage. Each heroine is an example of chastity, sometimes under inconvenient conditions. They are both extremely beautiful, and have no other attributes to interest us. The manly beauty of the hero, and his equivocal status as 'brother' of his lady-love, exposes him to the importunities of a princess who goes to extreme limits in her suit. The athletic ability of Theagenes is enhanced for Persiles by the annexation of the sports from *Aeneid* v. Each book starts *in medias res* and goes on to a vast recital of past events. The range of the Greek novel is from the Aegean to the extreme south of the known world, and that of the Spanish work is from the unknown north to Spain and Italy, the heroine being in each case a princess of the remotest regions. The first scene is on a wild sea-shore, among islands and robbers. Capture and massacres and escape follow, and then more capture and separation and reunion. To the barbarized Spaniard Antonio corresponds the barbarized Greek Knemon, both being fugitives as the result of crimes of violence. But this parallel can go on for ever, so continual are the coincidences. Whether Cervantes also consulted Achilles Tatius is the more doubtful because of the complete satisfaction he seemed to find in Heliodorus.

In addition to this supreme source, we have seen that Cervantes had in mind the *Aeneid* and reproduced with a difference the fifth book. He drew his northern geography from the spurious travels of the Zeni brothers, to which the date 1380 was wrongfully attached. He acknowledged the debt (iv. 13) in respect of the island of Frislanda. The notion that the northern seas were wholly occupied with islands came from poring over contemporary maps, such as those in Ramusio's volumes. Olaus Magnus gave him some notion of Vikings and sea-monsters. As for the customs of their presumable inhabitants, Cervantes obtained his material not from the north but from the west. His barbarians practise the rites and wear the clothing of Garcilaso de la Vega el Inca's American aborigines in the *Royal Commentaries*, published in 1609.

This date, 1609, is therefore to be attached to the opening chapters of the whole work, and it is valid also for the eleventh chapter of the third book, where the expulsion of the Moriscos is considered to be imminent. It is probable that the book was begun in 1609 and at least roughed out. It was far enough advanced in 1612 to be announced for future publication, and in 1615 it lacked only four months of completion. None the less, death prevented the author from perfecting his work, since his last chapters are hurried and infelicitous in the extreme. But while these dates may be looked upon with some confidence, they do not necessarily apply to other parts of the novel. It would seem that Cervantes swept the contents of his note-books into this compendious frame, with the result that the inset novelettes are of all three exemplary styles. Two of them (*Antonio the Barbarian* and *Renato*) refer to the latter years of Charles V, and the mage Soldino (iii. 18) is caused to prophesy the battles of Lepanto and Alcacerquibir (1571 and 1578). Despite that indication we are informed that Tasso's *Gerusalemme* has appeared (1584); in short, there is nothing to be obtained by attempting a chronology of these adventures.

Persiles enjoyed some favour in its time, and has always found admirers. Don Luis Fernández-Guerra held that it was a

'treasure of adventures and dramatic situations, of experience and philosophy, of masterly maxims, finished phrases, brilliant idioms, and of descriptions filled with the clearest and most enticing truth.'

'Azorín' has more recently felt the charm of the misty northern seas and the distant islands; he maintains also that the golden Cervantine prose reached its perfection in this book. These critics are concerned with details. They do not answer Mayans' charge that the principal theme is obscured by the episodes; but they invite us to enjoy the narrative as it comes. It is a bolder stroke to call this work, as Professor Farinelli has done, Cervantes' last romantic dream. The word 'romantic' has always had a fascination for this scholar, who thereby thrusts on one side the demand for perspective and proportion. It was Cervantes' intention to write a novel on the classical pattern not only of Heliodorus but, at a second remove, of Virgil; but we may admit that it was his pleasure to pour out on paper the varied content of his fancy, without considering sufficiently the unity and texture of the whole. His description of the northern islands corresponded to the prejudices of his age. Spaniards were prepared to accept many things as probable in distant lands which they would not allow in Spain; and it is in accordance with this prejudice that Cervantes' narrative is so firm and credible in the first half of the third book (in which the pilgrims cross from Lisbon to Valencia) but at once loses outline in Perpignan. In the far north anything might be true; but to consider his islands to be charming or his voyage to be an elegant progress, as Azorín does, is to dilute the author's text with too many of the reader's preferences.

The principal action is thin and is botched at the end. The hero and heroine are present throughout, and parts of the first, second, and fourth books are given to their affairs. But they are figures rendered pallid by their aureoles, and all their evolutions are the tritest commonplaces of romance. It is not so much a matter of proportion between the fable and the episodes, but of the insipidity of the fable itself. It is lost in a dim haze, so that only the interpolated episodes stand clearly before us. A similar affliction besets Cervantes' style. It does reach formal perfection in this novel, but it is so often applied to insignificant matter that the effect is hollow and dull.

It is then the inset stories that make the *Persiles*. These are of the utmost variety of theme and style, and are very variously placed in the common frame. The first book contains a group of four: *Antonio the Spanish Barbarian*, *Rutilio the Italian Dancer*, *Manuel de Sousa Coutinho or the enamoured Portuguese*, and the history of *Transila or jus primæ noctis*. The first is, for the most part, a realistic sketch based on pundonor, and it may have some autobiographical interest. There is Italian fantasy in the second, together with a copious injection of witchcraft. The third pokes fun at the Portuguese, who alone are capable of dying of love. The fourth is set in Ireland because its inverisimilitude would not permit a nearer approach to Spain. It introduces the spirited

Transila who objects to making her bridal bed common property, and it furnishes Cervantes with his Mauricio, an astrologer. The name is Irish, being that of Desmond Fitzmaurice of Munster, but the custom castigated derives from Garcilaso el Inca. In addition the author asks for our interest in lasciviousness as embodied in Rosamunda (the fair Rosamond of Woodstock), and slander personified in Clodio. They live up to their qualities, and each dies as the result of ingrained vice.

The second book is taken up with the love of King Policarpo for Sigismunda and that of Princess Sinforosa for Persiles, thus giving a typically Cervantine tangle. Then follows an immense recital of Persiles' adventures, with somewhat ironical comments by Mauricio, who finds the story long for an episode in an epic plot. It becomes a series of tableaux, since the author seems already to have lost interest in his hero. We hear of a wedding among fisherfolk, an allegorical boat-race, a dream, an unlucky king, a female pirate, and the taming of a modern Bucephalus. Witchcraft and astrology also thicken the soup, and at the end Cervantes throws in the story of *Renato and Eusebia* to show that a trial by battle may not justify the innocent.

It would seem from a passage in the third book (chapter 19) that Cervantes intended his heroes to move in an atmosphere charged with destiny. Hence the various witches: Rutilio's witch, Zenotia, the Jewess Julia. Mauricio makes prognostications by judicial astrology, and Soldino is a clairvoyant. The book opens with a false prophecy, which induces the barbarians to practise human sacrifice. So Persiles moves like Aeneas amid portents and wonders; but Cervantes employs the squalid machinery of omens and wizardry which may have seemed more plausible than that of Olympus in his age, but now unites improbability to nausea. This tendency towards the loathsome supernatural had been typical of the Spanish outlook from the days of Seneca and Lucan, and it was exemplified in Ercilla's *Araucana*, the greatest of Spanish epics and much admired by Cervantes.

To the third book the hero and heroine contribute only movement. We are on firm Cervantine ground so long as the party travels through the Spanish meseta, and the novelettes are numerous and good. Two are romantic: Feliciana de la Voz runs away from home to avoid an unwelcome suitor and Ambrosia Agustina does the same to recover the affections of her errant husband. From Giraldi Cinzio Cervantes obtained the motif of an enemy's magnanimity, when he shows how a noble Portuguese mother protected a suppliant even when she knew him to be her son's murderer. The story of *The Talaveran Wanton* recurs at intervals through the third and fourth books. She is a lively sinner, and her career might have borne the moral that the wages of sin are death, were it not for the princely intervention of Persiles. There is a brilliant sketch of rustic courtship by the Tagus, and an amusing affair of some students detected in obtaining alms under false pretences. On reaching Valencia Cervantes uses his knowledge of the Moorish descents on the exposed coast, with the connivance of local Moriscos.

Entering France midway in the book, the narrative loses this realism. We hear of a vengeful Scottish heroine, Ruperta, who enters a youth's chamber with intent to kill and remains to marry. Reaching Italy before the book closes, we find a country with recognizable sites and characteristics, but more ingenious and romanesque than Spain. It is the land of cunning intrigue and fit for Isabella Castrucho, who feigns demon-possession in order to baffle her father's favourite and be cured by the student of her own choice.

The last book is the weakest. It is devoted to clearing up the ends of the main action and some minor ones, and develops two new themes: that of the duke who falls in love with a portrait, and that of the Roman courtesan Hipólita. The description of her Renaissance elegance and lack of scruple is much more interesting than the use Cervantes has made of the trite Joseph and Zuleika motif.

This then is the work of which its author entertained such high hopes. Its models were the best that ancient epic or romance could provide, and it gave the writer scope to express all he remembered or imagined. A master's hand shaped the narratives and the prose, and many maxims and reflections serve to show his ripe experience of life. But the spectacle of unrelieved virtue in the main persons proves intolerable, and the work falls into fragments. It is then the exemplary novelist who emerges, in this last book as in his first, putting his hand to plots that are lifelike and some that are arbitrary. To the arbitrary he concedes, perhaps, too great a space, prompted by the tolerant yearnings of a green old age. For bad and good alike he devised happy endings, but the author of the third book has the keen sight and sure hand which fashioned *Rinconete* and *The Dogs' Colloquy*.

CERVANTES' LIFE

MIGUEL DE CERVANTES SAAVEDRA was born at Alcalá de Henares and baptized on 9 October 1547, son of Rodrigo de Cervantes, a surgeon, and Leonor de Cortinas. He had an elder brother, Rodrigo, and several sisters, among whom Andrea and Magdalena were frequently members of Miguel's household. His father does not seem to have been successful in his profession, and the boy's early life was spent at Sevilla, Madrid, and other places. Philip II's third queen, Isabel de Valois, died on 3 October 1568, and in the next year Cervantes contributed certain poems to a volume of her exequies issued by Juan López de Hoyos, the Latinist of the Studium of Madrid. In it Cervantes is described as a beloved pupil, the precise sense not being plain.

We next hear of Cervantes in Italy, on 22 December 1569. The cause is not known for certain, but a document dated 15 September 1569 condemns to ten years' exile and the loss of his right hand a Miguel de Cervantes who may well have been our author. He may have anticipated arrest. For a while he was servant to the young Giulio Acquaviva, later Cardinal, but he soon enlisted, and was on board the *Marquesa* at the battle of Lepanto (7 October 1571). He was suffering from fever that day, but insisted in taking part in the fighting, and received wounds in the chest and one which disabled his left hand. This left him maimed for life. His brother joined him, and both took part in operations in Corfu, at Navarino, and in Tunis, as well as passing some time in garrison in various Italian towns. He was recommended for promotion, and accordingly embarked with his brother on the *Sol* to press his claim in Spain. On 26 September 1575 the vessel was attacked and taken by three Turkish galleys off Les Saintes Maries. His captor was an Albanian renegade called Arnaut Mami.

Carried off to Algiers, Cervantes became the slave of Dali Mami. An exaggerated estimate of his importance resulted from perusal of the commendatory letters he carried, and he was held for a high ransom. In time the family contrived to recover Rodrigo, but had no funds for Miguel. Rodrigo returned to Spain in 1577 with a plan to secure a frigate to rescue such slaves as Miguel could secrete in Hassan's garden. The frigate came and was detected. Miguel Cervantes had already achieved a great exploit in concealing and provisioning the party for six months; he now took the whole blame on his own shoulders, despite threats of death, and thus protected his associates. He planned to escape to Oran in 1578, and in the next year he made another attempt to escape to Valencia, though the plan was wrecked by the perfidy of a traitor. In 1580 Cervantes was on the point of being dispatched to Constantinople when he was redeemed by Trinitarian monks. They happened to have money in hand because their offers for a certain Gerónimo Palafox were considered too low, but sufficient for Miguel de Cervantes.

He reached Madrid on 18 December 1580 and spent most of the next seven years there. He visited Portugal and Oran in 1581, but only on short missions. At Madrid he busied himself with the composition of plays and *La Galatea*. A daughter Isabel de Saavedra was born to him by an intrigue with a certain Ana Franca de Rojas, and on 12 December 1584 he married Catalina de Salazar Vozmediano y Palacios, a girl eighteen years his junior, who possessed a small property at Esquivias.

Preparations for the sailing of the Armada gave Cervantes a chance to enter the public service as commissary for provisions. He was so engaged in the autumn of 1587 and in 1588. A brush with the Dean and Chapter of Sevilla led to his temporary excommunication. Écija was his centre, but he removed to Sevilla after the defeat of the Armada. He was lucky enough to keep his post, but his salary was falling into arrears. In May 1590 he drew up a statement of his services and petitioned the King for any one of four American posts then vacant. This petition was rejected.

His arrears of pay amounted to 110,400 maravedis on 12 March 1591, but the peculations of an assistant brought his conduct under suspicion. The official accountants found Cervantes in deficit 27,046 maravedis. Other irregularities occurred to aggravate the case, but none the less Cervantes was instructed to collect, in 1594, two and a half million maravedis of arrears of taxation in the province of Granada. He encountered opposition from the taxpayers, and, attempting to use a bank for convenience of transmission to the Treasury, he was involved in the bankruptcy of Freire de Lima, of Sevilla. Cervantes was now unemployed, and was arrested and lodged in Sevilla jail in September 1597, being released on 1 December. There had been a mistake as to the sum in deficit for which surety was demanded. The next five years are very obscure, since Cervantes was living from hand to mouth and was continually harassed by demands from the Treasury. His brother Rodrigo was killed at the battle of Nieuwpoort in 1600, leaving arrears of pay which Miguel took years to recover.

After another arrest in 1602 Cervantes removed to Valladolid, then the capital of Spain. He completed *Don Quixote*, i, and published it in 1605. His livelihood seems to have come from commissions, and he continued to have difficulties with the Treasury. The death of a rake named Ezpeleta on the doorstep of his house led to the temporary arrest of the Cervantes family. They recovered their liberty, but the circumstances remained suspicious.

His daughter Isabel had removed to Madrid by 24 June 1608, and the family must have followed. A series of documents concerning her extend from this year to 1612, due to a triangular entanglement between her and Juan de Urbina and a certain Luis de Molina. In the end Urbina paid costs, while Molina became Isabel's husband. Cervantes does not appear as a principal in this affair. He was busy with literary projects: *The Exemplary Novels* (1613), *Voyage to Parnassus* (1614), *Don Quixote*, ii (1615), *Eight Comedies and Eight*

Interludes (1615), *Persiles* (posthumous, 1617). He enjoyed fame as an author and entered various literary academies frequented by Lope de Vega. His finances continued to be embarrassed, and he had to make use of his wife's interest. Her will in 1610 left most of her property away from him, but it was later revoked. In 1613 Cervantes took the robe of the Franciscan Tertiaries at Alcalá, by way of preparation for death. Death took him on 23 April 1616 (New Style), Shakespeare having died on the same date (Old Style). He was buried in the Trinitarian convent in the Calle de Cantarranas, his grave being left without a stone. No will has been found. His daughter lived until 1652.

WORKS OF CERVANTES

OCCASIONAL POEMS.

1569 Epistle to Cardinal Espinosa and other pieces on the death of Queen Isabel. 1577 Epistle to Mateo Vázquez. 1588 two odes on the Armada. 1593 *Jealousy* (ballad). 1595 Glosses of S. Jacinto. 1596 invectives against Medina Sidonia. 1598 poems on the death of Philip II. 1616 On the Ecstasy of St. Teresa.

Complimentary verses: 1577 to Ruffino de Chiambery. 1579 Antonio Veneziano. 1583, 1585, 1587 Padilla. 1584 Rufo's *Austriad.* 1586 López Maldonado. 1587 Barros. 1588 Díaz. 1596 Mosquera de Figueroa. 1602 Lope de Vega. 1605 Herrera. 1610 Hurtado de Mendoza. 1613 Barrio Angulo, Rosel. 1616 Yagüe de Salas, Alfonsa González.

NOVELS.

1585 *Galatea* (including the novelettes of *Lisandro* and *The two Friends,* with the *Song of Calliope*).

PLAYS.

c. 1585 *Numantia; The Traffic of Algiers;* and other plays lost or remodelled.

NOVELS.

1605, 1615 *Don Quixote,* i, ii (including, i, *Grisóstomo and Marcela, Cardenio, The Curious Impertinent, The captive Captain, The Muleteer, Fair Leandra;* and, ii, *Camacho's Wedding, Claudia Jerónima, The Moor Ricote*).

1613 *The Exemplary Novels* (*The liberal Lover, The Call of the Blood, Rinconete, The jealous Extremaduran, The Spanish Englishwoman, The illustrious Kitchen-wench, Tricked into Marriage, The Dogs' Colloquy, Licentiate Glass, The two Damsels, Lady Cornelia, The little Gipsy*) together with *The feigned Aunt* (1606).

POEM.

1614 *Voyage to Parnassus* and *Addendum to Parnassus.*

PLAYS.

1615 *Eight Comedies and Eight Interludes* (Comedies: *The House of Jealousy, Love's Labyrinth, The Bagnios of Algiers, The gallant Spaniard, The happy Ruffian, The Grand Sultana, The Comedy of Entertainment, Pedro de Urdemalas;* Interludes: *The widowed Ruffian, The Provosts of Daganzo, The Miracle Show, The Divorce Court Judge, The careful Guard, The jealous old Man, The Cave of Salamanca, The sham Biscayan*).

NOVEL.

1617 *Persiles and Sigismunda* (including *Antonio the Barbarian, Rutilio the Dancing-master, Transila, The enamoured Portuguese, Renato and Eusebia, Ortel Banedre, Feliciana de la Voz, The Wanton from Talavera, Ambrosia Agustina, Ruperta's Vengeance, Isabella Castrucho, Hippolita the Courtesan,* &c.).

UNFINISHED OR LOST.

Galatea, ii; *Weeks in the Garden; The famous Bernardo; The optical Illusion; Jerusalem; Amaranta; The unique and the charming Arsinda; The naval Battle; The Traffic of Constantinople and Death of Selim.*

INDEX